Art of Marketing

Published by :
Lotus Press Publishers & Distributors

Art of Marketing

Arun Mahapatra

LOTUS PRESS

4735/22, Prakash Deep Building
Ansari Road, Darya Ganj,
New Delhi - 110002

Lotus Press : Publishers & Distributors
Unit No. 220, 2nd Floor, 4735/22, Prakash Deep Building,
Ansari Road, Darya Ganj, New Delhi- 110002
Ph.: 23280047, 98118-38000
• E-mail : lotuspress1984@gmail.com
www.lotuspress.co.in

Art of Marketing

ISBN: 978-81-8382-206-0

Printed & Published by : **Lotus Press Publishers & Distributors,** New Delhi-02

PREFACE

Seen as a creative aspect of the business enterprise, marketing refers to all activities of businesses, such as advertising, distributing and selling, that have value for customers, clients, partners, and society at large. It is also concerned with anticipating the customers' future needs and wants, which are often discovered through market research.

Marketing is influenced by many of the social sciences, particularly psychology, sociology and economics. Anthropology is also a small, but growing influence. Market research underpins these activities. Through advertising, it is also related to many of the creative arts. The marketing literature is also infamous for re-inventing itself and its vocabulary according to the times and the culture.

The present text has been designed as a referral and guidebook for all in the marketing field, be they veterans or amateurs. The aim of the book is to not just guide readers through the whole science that comprises to make marketing what it is, but also enable readers to comprehend marketing in all its various complexities of competition, globalisation, enterprise expansion, etc. The agenda is to not just enable readers to grasp the essentials of marketing in the present time, but to understand what makes for good and successful marketing in an environment of a glut of products and services.

It is hoped that the comprehensive and incisive content of the book is enjoyed by all. Any suggestions for further improvement are most welcome.

Editor

CONTENTS

Other Books on

MANAGEMENT BOOKS

Lotus PRESS

Unit No. 220, 2nd Floor, 4735/22, Prakash Deep Building,
Ansari Road, Darya Ganj, New Delhi- 110002
Ph.: 32903912, 23280047, 9811594448
E-mail : lotuspress1984@gmail.com, www.lotuspress.co.in

1

INTRODUCTION TO MARKETING

The term Marketing developed from the original meaning which referred literally to going to market, as in shopping, or going to a market to sell goods or services. Marketing practice tends to be seen as a creative industry, which includes advertising, distribution and selling. It is also concerned with anticipating the customers' future needs and wants, which are often discovered through market research.

Marketing is influenced by many of the social sciences, particularly psychology, sociology, and economics. Anthropology is also a small, but growing influence. Market research underpins these activities. Through advertising, it is also related to many of the creative arts. The marketing literature is also infamous for re-inventing itself and its vocabulary according to the times and the culture.

MARKETING MIX

The Marketing Mix is generally accepted as the use and specification of the four P's describing the strategic position of a product in the marketplace. A marketing mix is the division of groups to make a particular product, by pricing, product, branding, place, and quality. Although some marketers have added other P's, such as personnel and packaging, the fundamentals of marketing typically identifies the four P's of the marketing mix as referring to:

- *Product:* A tangible object or an intangible service that is mass produced or manufactured on a large scale with a specific volume of units. Intangible products are often service based like the tourism industry and the hotel industry. Typical examples of a mass produced tangible object are the motor car and the disposable razor. A less obvious but ubiquitous mass produced service is a computer operating system.
- *Price:* The price is the amount a customer pays for the product. It is determined by. a number of factors including market share, competition, material costs, product identity and the customer's perceived value of the product. The business may increase or decrease the price of product if other stores have the same product.
- *Place:* Place represents the location where a product can be purchased. It is often referred to as the distribution channel. It can include any physical store as well as virtual stores on the Internet.
- *Promotion*: Promotion represents all of the communications that a marketer may use in the marketplace. Promotion has four distinct elements—advertising, public relations, word of mouth and point of sale. A certain amount of crossover occurs when promotion uses the four principal elements together, which is common in film promotion. Advertising covers any communication that is paid for, from television and cinema commercials, radio and Internet adverts through print media and billboards. One of the most notable means of promotion today is the

Promotional Product, as in useful items distributed to targeted audiences with no obligation attached. This category has grown each year for the past decade while most other forms have suffered. It is the only form of advertising that targets all five senses and has the recipient thanking the giver. Public relations are where the communication is not directly paid for and includes press releases, sponsorship deals, exhibitions, conferences, seminars or trade fairs and events. Word of mouth is any apparently informal communication about the product by ordinary individuals, satisfied customers or people specifically engaged to create word of mouth momentum. Sales staff often plays an important role in word of mouth and Public Relations.

Broadly defined, optimising the marketing mix is the primary responsibility of marketing. By offering the product with the right combination of the four P's marketers can improve their results and marketing effectiveness. Making small changes in the marketing mix is typically considered to be a tactical change. Making large changes in any of the four P's can be considered strategic. For example, a large change in the price, say from Rs. 525 to Rs. 950 would be considered a strategic change in the position of the product. However a change of Rs. 500 to Rs. 499 would be considered a tactical change, potentially related to a promotional offer.

The term "Marketing Mix" however, does not imply that the four P elements represent options. They are not trade-offs but are fundamental marketing issues that always need to be addressed. They are the fundamental actions that marketing requires whether determined explicitly or by default. As well as the standard four P's (Product, Pricing, Promotion and Placement), services marketing calls upon an extra three, totalling seven and known together as the extended marketing mix. These are:

- *People:* Any person coming into contact with customers can have an impact on overall satisfaction. Whether as part of a supporting service to a product or involved in a total service, people are particularly important because, in the customer's eyes, they are generally inseparable from the total service. As a result of this, they must be appropriately trained, well motivated and the right type of person. Fellow customers are also sometimes referred to under 'people', as they too can affect the customer's service experience, (e.g., at a sporting event).
- *Process:* This is the process(es) involved in providing a service and the behaviour of people, which can be crucial to customer satisfaction.
- *Physical evidence:* Unlike a product, a service cannot be experienced before it is delivered, which makes it intangible. This, therefore, means that potential customers could perceive greater risk when deciding whether to use a service. To reduce the feeling of risk, thus improving the chance for success, it is often vital to offer potential customers the chance to see what a service would be like. This is done by providing physical evidence, such as case studies, testimonials or demonstrations.

The following are the new four P's developed for the latest stage in Internet Marketing, which has been dubbed "Web 2.0".

- *Personalisation:* Customisation of products and services through the use of the Internet. But this concept is further extended with emerging social media and advanced algorithms. Emerging technologies will continue to push this idea forward.

- *Participation:* Allows the customer to participate in what the brand should stand for; the product directions and even which ads to run. This concept is laying the foundation for disruptive change through democratisation of information.
- *Peer-to-Peer:* This refers to customer networks and communities where advocacy happens. The historical problem with marketing is that it is "interruptive" in nature, trying to impose a brand on the customer. This is most apparent in TV advertising. These "passive customer bases" will ultimately be replaced by the "active customer communities". Brand engagement happens within those conversations. P2P is now being referred to as Social computing.
- *Predictive modelling:* This refers to algorithms that are being successfully applied in marketing problems (both a regression as well as a classification problem).

PRODUCT

A product is anything that can be offered to a market that might satisfy a want or need. In retailing, products are called merchandise. In manufacturing, products are purchased as raw materials and sold as finished goods. Commodities are usually raw materials such as metals and agricultural products, but a commodity can also be anything widely available in the open market.

Since 1575, the word "product" has referred to anything produced. Since 1695, the word has referred to "thing or things produced". The economic or commercial meaning of product was first used by political economist Adam Smith. In general usage, product may refer to a single item or unit, a group of equivalent products, a grouping of goods or services, or an industrial classification for the goods or services.

The specific meaning of generic product names varies over time and location. Some products such as bread, milk, and salt have been bartered or sold for centuries, but the meaning of "bread" or "milk" as a product varies. The technologies were not available for pasteurisation and homogenisation of milk until the 20th century, and these food processing technologies are not used worldwide. Bread varies by type of grain, specific recipe, and size of loaf. Certain products may be considered equivalent or interchangeable for the purposes of trade, record-keeping, and reporting, despite gradual changes in the product or variations among geographical locations.

The distinction between a new product and a minor modification to an existing product is not always clear. Certain products have a product life cycle in which the supply and demand for the product increases then decreases over time. The demand for certain food products such as bread will tend to increase with population, but the supply and demand for a specific brand of bread may decline over time. For example, in USA, a patent for a product is recognition that the product is new in a legal sense. "Utility patents may be granted to anyone who invents or discovers any new and useful process, machine, article of manufacture, or composition of matter, or any new and useful improvement thereof; design patents may be granted to anyone who invents a new, original, and ornamental design for an article of manufacture; and, plant patents may be granted to anyone who invents or discovers and asexually reproduces any distinct and new variety of plant." In business an equivalent, interchangeable or fungible product is defined by a company and its customers. A company's inventory is a set of physical products, or goods, that are usually recorded as counts of equivalent unique products. The equivalent unique products may be assigned a product code or item code on the company's records. If the company carries two brands, it may assign separate item codes to the brands, or it may use a single item code for both brands.

Product numbers in many businesses clearly identify the product by linking to a full description.

Product identification codes such as Universal Product Code, Global Trade Item Number and International Standard Book Number allow multiple businesses to use a single product identification code to indicate one unit of a mass-produced product.

Lot numbers, batch numbers or control numbers are used in manufacturing to sub-divide equivalent product by its manufacturing batch or run. The publishing page of a book lists the printing run that produced that unique book. Industries such as pharmaceuticals, food processing, and petroleum use some form of control number to sub-divide equivalent product for product testing or expiration dating. See also shelf life. Two separate lots may vary slightly, but they are not assigned separate product identification codes because the variation does not give them significantly different features or uses as products.

Branding

A brand is a name, term, design, symbol, or other feature that distinguishes products and services from competitive offerings. A brand represents the consumers' experience with an organisation, product, or service. A brand has also been defined as an identifiable entity that makes a specific value. Branding means creating reference of certain products in mind.

Some people distinguish the psychological aspect of a brand from the experiential aspect. The experiential aspect consists of the sum of all points of contact with the brand and is known as the brand experience. The psychological aspect, sometimes referred to as the brand image, is a symbolic construct created within the minds of people and consists of all the information and expectations associated with a product or service.

People engaged in branding seek to develop or align the expectations behind the brand experience, creating the impression that a brand associated with a product or service has certain qualities or characteristics that make it special or unique. A brand is therefore one of the most valuable elements in an advertising theme, as it demonstrates what the brand owner is able to offer in the marketplace. The art of creating and maintaining a brand is called brand management.

Careful brand management, supported by a cleverly crafted advertising campaign, can be highly successful in convincing consumers to pay remarkably high prices for products which are inherently extremely cheap to make. This concept, known as creating value, essentially consists of manipulating the projected image of the product so that the consumer sees the product as being worth the amount that the advertiser wants him/her to see, rather than a more logical valuation that comprises an aggregate of the cost of raw materials, plus the cost of manufacture, plus the cost of distribution. Modern value-creation branding-and-advertising campaigns are highly successful at inducing consumers to pay, for example, Rs. 500 for a T-shirt that cost a mere Rs. 75 to make, or Rs. 90 for a box of lunch that contains a few rupees of worth of items.

A brand which is widely known in the marketplace acquires brand recognition. When brand recognition builds up to a point where a brand enjoys a critical mass of positive sentiment in the marketplace, it is said to have achieved brand franchise. One goal in brand recognition is the identification of a brand without the name of the company present.

Consumers may look on branding as an important value added aspect of products or services, as it often serves to denote a certain attractive quality or characteristic. From the perspective of brand owners, branded products or services also command higher prices. Where two products resemble each other, but one of the products has no associated branding, people may often select the more expensive branded product on the basis of the quality of the brand or the reputation of the brand owner.

The brand name is often used interchangeably within "brand", although it is more correctly used to specifically denote written or spoken linguistic elements of any product. In this context a "brand name" constitutes a type of trademark, if the brand name exclusively identifies the brand owner as the commercial source of products or services. A brand owner may seek to protect proprietary rights in relation to a brand name through trademark registration.

The act of associating a product or service with a brand has become part of pop culture. Most products have some kind of brand identity, from common table salt to designer. How the brand owner wants the consumer to perceive the brand and by extension the branded company, organisation, product or service. The brand owner will seek to bridge the gap between the brand image and the brand identity. Brand identity is fundamental to consumer recognition and symbolises the brand's differentiation from competitors.

MARKETING COMMUNICATIONS

Marketing communications breaks down the strategies involved with marketing messages into categories based on the goals of each message. There are distinct stages in converting strangers to customers that govern the communication medium that should be used.

Advertising

- Paid form of public presentation and expressive promotion of ideas.
- Aimed at masses.
- Manufacturer may determine what goes into advertisement.
- Pervasive and impersonal medium.

Functions and advantages of successful advertising

- Task of the salesman made easier.

Objectives

- Maintain demand for well-known goods.
- Introduce new and unknown goods.
- Increase demand for well-known goods/products/ services.
- Create awareness.

Requirements of a good advertisement

- Attract attention (awareness).
- Stimulate interest.
- Create a desire.
- Bring about action.

Eight steps in an advertising campaign

- Market research.
- Setting out aims.
- Budgeting.

- Choice of media (television, newspaper/magazines, radio, web, outdoor).
- Choice of actors (New Trend).
- Design and wording.
- Co-ordination.
- Test results.

Personal sales

Oral presentation given by a salesperson who approaches individuals or a group of potential customers:

- Live, interactive relationship.
- Personal interest.
- Attention and response.
- Interesting presentation.

Sales promotion

Short-term incentives to encourage buying of products:

- Instant appeal.
- Anxiety to sell.

An example is coupons or a sale. People are given an incentive to buy, but this does not build customer loyalty or encourage future repeat buys. A major drawback of sales promotion is that it is easily copied by competition. It cannot be used as a sustainable source of differentiation.

Marketing Public Relations (MPR)

- Stimulation of demand through press release giving a favourable report to a product.
- Higher degree of credibility.
- Effectively news.
- Boosts enterprise's image.

Customer Focus

Many companies today have a customer focus. This implies that the company focuses its activities and products on consumer demands. Generally there are three ways of doing this: *the customer-driven approach, the sense of identifying market changes and the product innovation approach.*

In the consumer-driven approach, consumer wants are the drivers of all strategic marketing decisions. No strategy is pursued until it passes the test of consumer research. Every aspect of a market offering, including the nature of the product itself, is driven by the needs of potential consumers. The starting point is always the consumer. The rationale for this approach is that there is no point spending research and development funds developing products that people will not buy. History attests to many products that were commercial failures in spite of being technological breakthroughs.

A formal approach to this customer-focused marketing is known as SIVA (Solution, Information, Value, Access). This system is basically the four Ps renamed and reworded to provide a customer focus. The SIVA Model provides a demand/customer centric version alternative to the well-known four Ps supply side model (product, price, place, promotion) of marketing management.

Product	→	Solution
Promotion	→	Information
Price	→	Value
Place	→	Access

The four elements of the SIVA model are:

1. *Solution:* How appropriate is the solution to the customer's problem/need?

2. *Information:* Does the customer know about the solution? If so, how and from whom do they know enough to let them make a buying decision?
3. *Value:* Does the customer know the value of the transaction, what it will cost, what are the benefits, what might they have to sacrifice, what will be their reward?
4. *Access:* Where can the customer find the solution? How easily/locally/remotely can they buy it and take delivery?

Product Focus

In a product innovation approach, the company pursues product innovation, then tries to develop a market for the product. Product innovation drives the process and marketing research is conducted primarily to ensure that profitable market segment(s) exist for the innovation. The rationale is that customers may not know what options will be available to them in the future so we should not expect them to tell us what they will buy in the future. However, marketers can aggressively over-pursue product innovation and try to overcapitalise on a niche. When pursuing a product innovation approach, marketers must ensure that they have a varied and multi-tiered approach to product innovation. It is claimed that if Thomas Edison depended on marketing research he would have produced larger candles rather than inventing light bulbs. Many firms, such as research and development focused companies, successfully focus on product innovation. Many purists doubt whether this is really a form of marketing orientation at all, because of the ex post status of consumer research. Some even question whether it is marketing.

– An emerging area of study and practice concerns internal marketing, or how employees are trained and managed to deliver the brand in a way that positively impacts the acquisition and retention of customers (employer branding).

- Diffusion of innovations research explores how and why people adopt new products, services and ideas.
- A relatively new form of marketing uses the Internet and is called Internet marketing or more generally e-marketing, affiliate marketing, desktop advertising or online marketing. It tries to perfect the segmentation strategy used in traditional marketing. It targets its audience more precisely, and is sometimes called personalised marketing or one-to-one marketing.
- With consumers' eroding attention span and willingness to give time to advertising messages, marketers are turning to forms of permission marketing such as branded content, custom media and reality marketing.
- The use of herd behaviour in marketing.

2

CONCEPT OF MARKETING

Marketing is inherently multidimensional. As such, it is practised and studied from many distinct points of view, with varying means and toward different ends. Perhaps inevitably, a variety of definitions of marketing have emerged and evolved. Any academic at least consensus on defining marketing appears to be of comparatively recent vintage. The process definition of marketing reflects that marketing is concerned with the relationships between buyers and sellers within the process of exchange of economic products and services. This definition of marketing as a process is also known as the classical or narrow definition of marketing.

Marketing has, quite distinctly, been described as a business function and also as a business philosophy. As an example of the latter, consider for instance Baker defining marketing as:

> "Marketing is a very simple philosophy which requires producers to start with the identification and specification of consumer needs and the mobilise their companies' assets and resources to achieve a mutually satisfying exchange relationship from which both parties derive the benefits they are seeking".

As well as the management philosophy of marketing, Kotier stresses its social side:

> "Marketing is a social and managerial process by which individuals and groups obtain what they need and want through creating, offering, and exchanging products of value with others".

Despite the convergent nature of such definitions, the marked lack of consensus among the various authors remains. One could venture for explanations in that:

— By contrast to most other disciplines, notably the physical sciences and in some cases the "behavioural sciences, marketing has no recognised central theoretical basis.

— Marketing is a multidimensional phenomenon, combining the philosophy of business as well as its practice.

The classical definition of marketing clearly provides that marketing is managed within the marketing departments in the various business organisations, as it is concerned with the physical movement of economic goods and services. However, some of the shortcomings of approaching marketing as a process in the classical sense include:

— An overvaluation of the role of the physical distribution and of the marketing channels.

— The omission of government and non-profit organisations.

— Inadequate emphasis being ascribed in the importance of the procedure of Exchange between buyers and sellers.

— The marketing environment of the organisation is not considered.

The broader, modern definition of describing marketing as a process allows for escaping several pitfalls associated with the classical definition. In terms of the broader definition, the organisation achieves its goals by satisfying its customers.

ORIGIN OF MARKETING

The origins of marketing can be found in the process of people's exchange of one good for another. Before the Industrial Revolution, exchanges of goods were limited, as people did not have many items to trade. An early framework on the evolution of marketing since the industrial revolution is Keith's. According to him, there are three distinct central stages; the production era, the sales era and the marketing era. This framework has been widely accepted for a number of years, and is presented in several introductory marketing textbooks. Far from being an alternative definition of marketing, the marketing concept is "a way of thinking—a management philosophy guiding an organisation's overall activities [affecting] all the efforts of the organisation, not just its marketing activities". Recently, the marketing concept has become the way of thinking where the customer is located at the centre. This constitutes a radical departure from Henry Ford's marketing philosophy in the early 1900s, epitomised by his famous "the customers can have any colour car they want as long as it is black." Before the evolution of the American economy into a consumer society in the 1950s, marketing was primarily seen in the terms of selling, and the focal point for companies was products, not customers. Emerging first in the General Electric Company in 1952, the marketing concept has been consistently redefined over the past four decades. The landmark General Electric Company annual report announcing a new management philosophy stated that:

> "[The concept]... introduces the marketing man at the beginning rather than at the end of the production cycle and integrates marketing into each phase of business. Thus, marketing, through its studies and research, will establish for the engineer, the design and manufacturing man, what the customer wants in a given product, what price he is willing to pay, and where and when it will be wanted. Marketing will have

> the authority in product planning, production scheduling and inventory control, as well as in sales distribution and servicing for the product".

This radical step in the business world led various authors to further indulge in the marketing concept and consequently academic literature has gained new terms and views. The earliest response to business action was from Peter Drucker suggesting that the purpose of business should be to create and retain satisfied customers. Felton stressed the importance of integration and coordination of all the marketing functions, defining the marketing concept as "a corporate state of mind that insists on the integration and coordination of all the marketing functions, which, in turn, are melded with all other corporate functions, for the basic purpose of producing maximum long-range corporate profits." Keith's article still remains one of the significant commentaries as to the application of the marketing concept in practice. Keith described the changing attitudes on marketing as the marketing revolution, stressing that the business world now accepted the idea that the consumer, not the company, is at the centre. He examined the evolution of the Pillsbury Company in four stages, from production oriented to sales oriented, moving on to a marketing oriented state, the latter based on the idea that "marketing begins and ends with consumers". Finally, the fourth stage of this marketing revolution is marketing control which aims that marketing will become the basic motivating force for the entire corporation—from finance to sales and to production—to satisfy the needs and desires of the consumer.

Due to its highlighting of the sharp contrast between selling and marketing concepts, Levitt's 'Marketing Myopia' made a big contribution to the marketing literature. "The difference between marketing and selling is more than semantic. Selling focuses on the needs of seller, marketing on the needs of buyer. Selling is preoccupied with the seller's need to convert his product into cash; marketing with the idea of satisfying the needs of the customer by means of the product and the whole cluster of things associated with creating, delivering and finally consuming it".

Levitt underscored that the reason for the demise of many failing or declining industries was their product, rather than customer orientation. "The history of every dead and dying 'growth' industry shows a self-deceiving cycle of bountiful expansion and undetected decay". For Levitt, the presence of the following four conditions would usually guarantee this outcome:

1. The belief that growth is assured by an expansion and a more affluent population.
2. The belief that there is no competitive substitute for the industry's major product.
3. Too much faith in mass production and in the advantages of rapidly declining unit costs as output rises.
4. Preoccupation with a product that lends itself to carefully controlled scientific experimentation, improvement, and manufacturing cost reduction.

SCOPE OF MARKETING

Kotier and Levy initiated a new dimension suggesting that the marketing concept must be broadened to include nonbusiness organisations (for instance religious outfits, police departments, museums and public schools), as they too have products and consumers and they already employed some marketing tools. Therefore, "All organisations must develop appropriate products to serve their sundry consuming groups and must use modern tools of communication to reach their consuming publics.

The business heritage of marketing provides a useful set of concepts for guiding all organisations". Nonbusiness organisations are involved with marketing, and "the choice facing those who manage nonbusiness organisations is not whether to market or not to market, for no organisation can avoid marketing. The choice is whether do it well or poorly, and on this necessity the case for organisational marketing is basically founded".

In addition to broadening the range of organisations for which marketing is relevant, they also suggested that the concepts of products and consumers must be broadened. In his discussion of the changing boundaries of marketing Lazer denoted that these now extend beyond the profit motive, involving ethics, values, responsibilities and marketing-government relationships. He posed the question "What are the boundaries of marketing in modern society?" to which he suggested that we need to know that " what is required is a broader perception and definition of marketing than has hitherto been the case-one that recognises marketing's societal dimensions and perceives of marketing as more than just a technology of the firm".

On the broadening the concept of marketing, Kotier & Levy were initially censured on a number of counts: Marketing must be "deepened" as well as broadened. Furthermore, "not all exchanges are marketing exchanges; marketing will cover only the resolving of the economics needs and wants in society... [therefore] marketing will not include exchanges in noneconomic areas where participants are non-marketing institutions such as churches, welfare agencies, and cultural agencies". It is also possible to maintain that the marketing concept would result in the shifting of focus away from the product, design, development and manufacture and would not let the companies be successful on product innovation. Moreover, "the marketing concept is not applicable to two broad classes of producers because of the personal values and social norms that characterise the production process. These two types of producers are the 'artists' and the 'ideologists'".

Naturally, Kotier and Levy responded vigorously to subsequent criticism, taking issue first with Luck. Luck had proposed that marketing must be limited to those business processes and activities that ultimately result in a market transaction. Kotier & Levy ascribed a new form of myopia to Luck, suggesting that "the crux of marketing lies in a general idea of exchange rather than the narrower thesis of market transactions... [whilst] exchange involves two (or more) parties who voluntarily agree to enter into a 'trading' relationship". Other scholars rallying in support of Kotier & Levy include Lavidge who insisted that " the areas in which marketing people can, and must, be of service to society have broadened. In addition marketing's functions have been broadened. Marketing no longer can be defined adequately in terms of the activities involved in buying, selling, and transporting goods and services".

In addition, Lavidge stated his belief that marketing people have not only the opportunity but also a "responsibility" to serve society. As such responsibilities he propagated

- The reduction of marketing abuses and upgrading standards.
- To help in mitigating and ultimately eliminating the effects of poverty.
- To aid in improving the marketing of social and cultural services.
- To develop international marketing institutions which will contribute to improved.

— Utilisation and distribution of the world's resources and, to world peace.

Ferber also agreed on the broadening of the marketing concept saying that integration and diversification are the key words of marketing and that marketing will ultimately diversify into the social and the public policy fields.

Kotier & Zaltman later repeated the arguments on "social marketing". Their description of social marketing states that it is the design, implementation, and control of programmes calculated to influence the acceptability of social ideas and involving considerations of product planning, pricing, communication, distribution, and marketing research:

In the same issue of the *Journal of Marketing* where Kotler's and Zaltman's work had appeared, a number of other articles examined the relationship of marketing to social marketing and environmental management. Marketing tools and planning were applied to the fund-raising campaign of a national charity, aspects of the health service, population problems, and recycling solid wastes.

Bartels departure suggested a distinct broadening of the scope of marketing practice and therefore of "the concept of marketing, with the term of social marketing designating the application of marketing techniques to nonmarketing fields".

The proliferation of new ideas on the issues led Luck to express his "personal confusion regarding the meaning of 'social marketing' [and his] uncomfortable feeling about the identity of marketing". However, the brimming process continued unabated with Hunt identifying the micro/macro, profit/non-profit sector and positive/ normative dimensions of marketing, whilst contrasting that if marketing is to be restricted to only profit/micro/

normative dimensions, then in his opinion marketing is not a science.

In the meantime, Kotier restated his original ideas as a "generic" concept of marketing, pointing out that the core concept of marketing is the transaction. As a transaction Kotier defines almost any exchange of the values occurring not only between buyers and sellers or organisations and clients, but also between any two parties. In fact, "the things-of-values need not be limited to goods, services, and money; they include other resources such as time, energy, and feelings". In the same article he also categorised the marketing activities in the light of broadening of marketing; "Generic marketing further implies the marketing activity can be classed according to target market (marketing directed to supporters, employees, suppliers, agents, consumers, general public, special public, government, and competitors); the product (goods, services, organisations, person, places, and ideas) and the marketer (business, political, social, religious, cultural, and knowledge organisations".

Herein the evolution of what was later to become one of the most influential sects in the contemporary evaluation of the marketing concept continues by further advancing marketing within the context of exchange theory. Having first described marketing as an exchange, the authors continued broadening the concept of marketing by proposing that in that sense buyers are marketers too. For Bagozzi, social marketing, as a subset of the generic concept of marketing should in fact approach the creation and resolution of exchanges in social relationships with greater precision. He points to what in his opinion is a misdirected focus by marketers on, primarily, the direct transfers of tangible entities between two parties. In an extended discussion on the various types of exchanges, Bagozzi highlights a number of aspects indicative of the multidimensional nature of the actual marketing exchanges, where not only more than two parties may participate, but in addition there also is ample evidence to suggest that their character is rather indirect in that they involve intangible and symbolic aspects as well. Hence the meaning of exchange should not be limited within exchanges of market value but it should actually incorporate any type of social exchange. In fact Bagozzi has gone as far as to suggest in his conclusion that "exchange is a central concept in marketing" whose usefulness could extend as serving as "the foundation for that elusive 'general theory of marketing"'.

Within the foundations of the preceding analysis of exchanges, Pandya & Dholakia, have pointed out that the economic structure of contemporary societies can be captured in four types of institutions; households, private firms, public enterprises and government institutions. Trades and transfers are exchanges and could take one of three principal forms; market exchange, reciprocal exchange and redistributive exchange. The institutional framework, based on the political economy approach, presents an embedded view of exchange where households, private firms, public enterprises and government institutions are linked by reciprocal, redistributive and market exchanges. Clearly therefore, societies with a different and changing mix of institutions will have different patterns of exchange, which supports the view that the meaning of the exchange is inherently and inevitably different in each society.

Nichel's empirical study on the conceptual conflicts of marketing targeted 100 marketing professors obtaining a response rate of 74%. His results showed 95% of the respondents believing that the scope of marketing should be broadened to include nonbusiness organisations, 93% of them as agreeing that marketing is not concerned solely with economic goods and services, whilst 83% of the educators believed that activities other than those whose ultimate result is a market transaction should be included in the domain of marketing. Recapitulating, it was the reorganisation of the General Electric Company in the early 1950s that sparked off a corporate business philosophy later to become known as the marketing concept.

Its definition, limitations, implements and general understanding of it was to last well into the early 1970s. Because the marketing concept was understood in different ways, its application was far from smooth, whilst it confused both managers and educators. The marketing concept has been heavily criticised since its early 1950s appearance, and it is unlikely that it will remain entirely uncontroversial. Some of its critics believe that it has been so widely misunderstood that it not only needs to be radically reviewed but that also "it is... time that we relearn the marketing concept". Despite whatever weaknesses however, it made managers realise that selling is different than marketing, that customer wants and needs must be the focus point, and that organisations should try to provide goods and services that satisfy customers' needs through a co-ordinated set of activities and integrated efforts that lead the organisation to achieve its goals.

IMPLEMENTING MARKETING CONCEPT

The marketing concept is fundamentally a business philosophy that includes customer orientation and integrated organisation activities in achieving organisations' goals. The marketing concept leads an organisation to achieve its goals by providing for customer satisfaction. Many authors have defined the marketing concept in different ways, but perhaps the one, which is widely recognised, has that,

> "The marketing concept holds that the key achieving organisational goals consists of being more effective than competitors in integrating marketing activities toward determining and satisfying the needs and wants of target markets".

The marketing concept is based on four main pillars; market focus, customer orientation, coordinated marketing and profitability.

- *Market Focus*: Before companies concentrate on customer satisfaction, they must find the target market in which they can operate and achieve what they want. Companies may essentially not operate in each market and satisfy all different needs. Therefore, defining the target market is the first step of applying and implementing the marketing concept.
- *Customer Orientation:* Most of the organisations have apparently failed to implement the marketing concept, for their understanding of it remains essentially the making a product that they believe customers need. Product-oriented companies fail to ask customers what they want and need. What a General Motors executive said on the issue some years ago constitutes a prime example in understanding the way that product-oriented companies operate; "How can the public know what kind of car they want until we have invented it?" McKitterick, a former president of General Electric, explains how companies must see that "the principal task of the marketing function in a management concept is not so much to be skilful in making the customer do what suits the interests of the business as to be skilful in conceiving and then making the business do what suits the interests of the customer".

- *Coordinated Marketing:* Coordinated marketing means that marketing functions such as product management, sales, marketing research, advertising must be integrated among themselves, and also that the marketing function must be integrated with the other functions of the organisation in order to enhance the organisation's total effectiveness. Coordinated marketing stresses that all functions of the organisations must work like in one body. This may only be executed successfully when the executives of the organisation understand the importance of this notion and can make it work in the organisation.
- *Profitability:* The marketing concept means not only satisfying customers but also achieving the goals of the organisation that would allow it to stay in business in the long-term. The aim of the company is not to make money; it is to find a profitable way to satisfy customers. The way achieve this aim is by focusing on profit rather than sales-volume.

Here the four pillars of the marketing concept have been summarised. Implementation of the marketing concept however is a complicated process. It involves identification of the target market, ascertaining what customers want and need, creating the right products and achieving organisational goals. This may only succeed if all functions within the organisation work harmoniously together and if the organisations' management and employees believe and observe this philosophy in the process of leading the organisation to achieve its goals. According to Kotier however, very few companies have successfully implemented the marketing concept. "Most companies have not arrived at full marketing maturity. They think they have marketing because they have a marketing vice-president, product managers, a salesforce, advertising budgets, and so on.

But a marketing department does not assure a market-oriented company".

CRITICS OF THE MARKETING CONCEPT

The marketing concept has been criticised on the following grounds.

The marketing concept discourages product innovation; Perhaps the most widely criticised aspect of the marketing concept is the suggestion that organisations must be customer oriented to effect new products meeting customers' needs and wants. Buyer models implicitly assumed in the marketing concept have been based on the basis of rational decision making hypothesis, in particular that;

(a) Consumers have goals/wants to satisfy which have low cost for them.

(b) The wants and needs of consumers can be identified by researchers from how people say and express their goals.

Kaldor says that customers do not always know their needs and cannot be always rational in the sense of their future needs. He also claims that the marketing concept is an inadequate prescription for marketing strategy, because it ignores the creative abilities of organisations. Houston has suggested that "rather than describing marketing concept as an 'inadequate prescription it would be better to describe it as an 'incomplete prescription'. The marketing concept focuses the marketer's attention on the customer but does not tell the marketer to disregard his/her unique capabilities and resources when deciding how to serve the customer's needs and wants best".

It has been argued that the marketing concept discourages major product innovation leading organisations away from major product innovation towards low risk product changes. In fact, Bennett & Cooper blame the marketing concept in the sense that "the marketing concept has diverted our attention from the product and its manufacture; instead we have focused our strategy on responses to market wants and have become preoccupied with advertising, selling and promotion". Houston's understanding however is somewhat different. "The marketing concept does not urge us to depend solely on marketing research for guidance in new product research... the marketing concept does not consist of advertising, selling, and promotion. It is willingness to recognise and understand the customer's needs and wants, and a willingness to adjust any of marketing mix elements, including product, to satisfy those needs and wants".

Bennet & Cooper argued that the marketing concept will result in the killing of new products. In order to encourage significant product innovation they propose "The product value concept" in their second article. "The product value concept is a business orientation that recognises that product value is the key to profits. It stresses competing on the basis of customer need satisfaction with superior, higher value products. Value depends on the customer's perception of the product attributes, which are largely a function of the firm's technological, design and manufacturing strengths and skills".

Bennet & Cooper also argue that "technology push" models has given way to "market pull models" that used to provide little encouragement for technological discoveries, inventions or significant breakthroughs. They maintain that market pull models constitute the antithesis of the technology push model. Riesz agrees that the shift from "science pushes" to "market pull" can have negative effects on the corporate strategy of the firms and the public policy of the governments.

In contrast to Bennett & Cooper, and Riesz arguments, Kiel states that the defence of marketing is based on three main arguments; "Firstly, marketing pull and technological push are not opposing, mutually exclusive paths to innovation. These concepts have become strawmen built upon a misunderstanding of the nature and roles of science and technology. Secondly, considerable empirical evidence on the innovation process proves that market-related forces are the primary influence on technological innovation. Thirdly, the view of the marketing concept put forward by its detractors is overly simplistic".

In addition, Kiel proposes that the marketing concept can work in conjunction with R & D efforts to produce innovation. He enlists support for his argument from an empirical study claiming market related forces to be the primary influence on innovation.

Some empirical studies support such claims that the marketing concept can work successfully on new product planning. Lawton & Parasuman in fact have proposed that there is no evidence to support that the adaptation of the marketing concept should influence new product planning. Recently Kodama has stressed that it is "the market [that] drives the R & D agenda, not the other way around". He has also pointed out that companies that rely on a technology strategy that no longer works in a such a fast changing environment, can not be successful in the longer term, because a single breakthrough technology focuses on the R & D effort too narrowly and ignores the possibilities of combining technologies. Therefore, companies need to have both the breakthrough and the "technology fusion" approaches in their technology strategies.

3

DEVELOP YOUR OWN MARKETING STRATEGY

A marketing strategy is a process that can allow an organisation to concentrate its limited resources on the greatest opportunities to increase sales and achieve a sustainable competitive advantage. A marketing strategy should be centred around the key concept that customer satisfaction is the main goal. A marketing strategy is most effective when it is an integral component of corporate strategy, defining how the organisation will successfully engage customers, prospects, and competitors in the market arena. corporate strategies, corporate missions, and corporate goals. As the customer constitutes the source of a company's revenue, marketing strategy is closely linked with sales. A key component of marketing strategy is often to keep marketing in line with a company's overarching mission statement.

SECTORIAL TACTICS AND ACTIONS

A marketing strategy can serve as the foundation of a marketing plan. A marketing plan contains a set of specific actions required to successfully implement a marketing strategy. For example: "Use a low-cost product to attract consumers. Once our organisation, via our low-cost product, has established a relationship with consumers, our organisation will sell additional, higher-margin products and services that enhance the consumer's interaction with the low-cost product or service."

A strategy consists of a well thought out series of tactics to make a marketing plan more effective. Marketing strategies serve as the fundamental underpinning of marketing plans designed to fill market needs and reach marketing objectives. Plans and objectives are generally tested for measurable results.

A marketing strategy often integrates an organisation's marketing goals, policies, and action sequences (tactics) into a cohesive whole. Similarly, the various strands of the strategy, which might include advertising, channel marketing, internet marketing, promotion and public relations can be orchestrated. Many companies cascade a strategy throughout an organisation, by creating strategy tactics that then become strategy goals for the next level or group. Each one group is expected to take that strategy goal and develop a set of tactics to achieve that goal. This is why it is important to make each strategy goal measurable.

Marketing strategies are dynamic and interactive. They are partially planned and partially unplanned.

TYPES OF STRATEGIES

Marketing strategies may differ depending on the unique situation of the individual business. However there are a number of ways of categorising some generic strategies. A brief description of the most common categorising schemes is presented below:

- *Strategies based on market dominance*: In this scheme, firms are classified based on their market share or dominance of an industry. Typically there are three types of market dominance strategies:

- Leader
- Challenger
- Follower

- *Porter generic strategies*: trategy on the dimensions of strategic scope and strategic strength. Strategic scope refers to the market penetration while strategic strength refers to the firm's sustainable competitive advantage.
  - Product differentiation
  - Market segmentation
- *Innovation strategies*: This deals with the firm's rate of the new product development and business model innovation. It asks whether the company is on the cutting edge of technology and business innovation. There are three types:
  - Pioneers
  - Close followers
  - Late followers
- *Growth strategies*: In this scheme we ask the question, "How should the firm grow?" There are a number of different ways of answering that question, but the most common gives four answers:
  - Horizontal integration
  - Vertical integration
  - Diversification
  - Intensification

A more detailed scheme uses the categories:

- Prospector
- Analyser

- — Defender
- — Reactor
- — *Marketing warfare strategies*: This scheme draws parallels between marketing strategies and military strategies.

STRATEGIC MODELS

Marketing participants often employ strategic models and tools to analyse marketing decisions. When beginning a strategic analysis, the 3Cs can be employed to get a broad understanding of the strategic environment. An Ansoff Matrix is also often used to convey an organisation's strategic positioning of their marketing mix. The four P's can then be utilised to form a marketing plan to pursue a defined strategy.

There are a many companies especially those in the Consumer Package Goods (CPG) market that adopt the theory of running their business centred around Consumer, Shopper and Retailer needs. Their marketing departments spend quality time looking for "growth opportunities" in their categories by identifying relevant insights (both mindsets and behaviours) on their target consumers, shoppers and retail partners. These growth opportunities emerge from changes in market trends, segment dynamics changing and also internal brand or operational business challenges. The marketing team can then prioritise these growth opportunites and begin to develop strategies to exploit the opportunities that could include new or adapted products, services as well as changes to the four P's.

Real-life marketing primarily revolves around the application of a great deal of common-sense; dealing with a limited number of factors, in an environment of imperfect information and limited resources complicated by uncertainty and tight timescales. Use of classical marketing techniques, in these circumstances, is inevitably partial and uneven.

Thus, for example, many new products will emerge from irrational processes and the rational development process may be used (if at all) to screen out the worst non-runners. The design of the advertising, and the packaging, will be the output of the creative minds employed; which management will then screen, often by 'gut-reaction', to ensure that it is reasonable.

For most of their time, marketing managers use intuition and experience to analyse and handle the complex, and unique, situations being faced; without easy reference to theory. This will often be 'flying by the seat of the pants', or 'gut-reaction'; where the overall strategy, coupled with the knowledge of the customer which has been absorbed almost by a process of osmosis, will determine the quality of the marketing employed. This, almost instinctive management, is what is sometimes called 'coarse marketing'; to distinguish it from the refined, aesthetically pleasing, form favoured by the theorists.

OBJECTIVES OF MARKETING STRATEGIES

A marketing strategy is a broad directional statement indicating how the marketing objectives will be achieved. It provides the method for accomplishing the objectives. While marketing objectives are specific, quantifiable, and measurable, marketing strategies are descriptive.

Within your plan, the marketing strategies represent a first overview of various marketing elements and how they will be utilised to achieve the marketing objectives. The most commonly addressed strategy issues are as follows, though you should consider what is most appropriate for your particular situation:

1. Building the market versus stealing market share.
2. National, regional, or local markets.
3. Seasonality.
4. Spending.
5. Competition.
6. Target market.
7. Product.
8. Naming.
9. Packaging.
10. Pricing.
11. Distribution/penetration or coverage.
12. Personal selling/service/operations.
13. Promotion/events.
14. Advertising message.
15. Advertising media.
16. Internet media.
17. Merchandising.
18. Public relations.
19. Marketing research and testing (R&T .

In some cases, the marketing strategies section of your plan may be the only place where some of these issues are discussed directly, such as building a market or spending. In such cases, the strategies you develop here will provide guideposts for a variety of tactical decisions later in the plan. For example, you may establish a market building strategy with the introduction of a new product. Such a strategy provides the context for advertising and promotion plans, among others, as you will need to build a high level of awareness and generate trial through a high level of activity for your new product.

You will notice that many of the marketing elements addressed in the marketing strategies are reconsidered from a specific tactical perspective later in the plan. The marketing strategies developed here serve as a reference for the tactical tools that follow. They provide the general strategic direction to accomplish the marketing objectives, but they do not include such specifics as "use television," for example, which belongs in the tactical media segment of the marketing plan.

Alternative Strategies

Build the market or steal market share

A critical strategic decision facing all marketers writing a plan is whether to build the market or steal share from competitors in order to achieve sales goals. The information regarding product awareness and attributes in your business review, and the product life cycle specifically, will help provide answers to this fundamental question.

A situation with a relatively new product where the current user base is small, the potential user base is quite large, and there is little competition often requires a "build the market" strategy. Many times, the company that creates the market maintains the largest market share long into the future. You have to develop a need for the product and then convince a target market to purchase your particular brand. Many companies intentionally take a "second to market" product development strategy. They allow someone else to invest in building the market, and then introduce their brand.

In a situation where the product is a mature one with minimal growth (i.e., few new customers entering the marketplace), stealing market share from competitors is often called for. In this situation you have to convince product category users that your product is superior to that of your competition. In some cases, the market may be growing, which allows your firm to grow along with it. In this case, the question becomes, "Is the market growing at the same rate I want to grow?" If the answer is no, then you will still need to steal share from your competition. All of these scenarios would be described in the market share strategy.

The decision of whether to build the market or steal share must be made up front in your marketing strategy section, as this is a very fundamental strategic decision that will affect all other areas of the marketing plan. A stealing share strategy, such as "steal market share from the leading competitor," requires that your company's target market definitions closely approximate those of the current market leader's customer profile. Also, the advertising will most likely communicate benefits or an image of your product that the market leader doesn't possess. To the contrary, a "build the market" strategy often requires first educating new customers about the benefits of product usage and then convincing them to use your company's products.

National, Regional, and Local Market Strategies

This marketing strategy category is often overlooked by the national and regional marketer. This strategy helps the marketer determine whether there will be a core national marketing plan or a combination of national, regional, and local marketing plans. Having a combination of plans requires a lot of work, but it is usually worth the effort. This strategy recognises regional DMA (Designated Market Area or television viewing area) and even local trading area differences by allowing for the application of specific territorial marketing programmes.

If you are a retailer, for example, you may have a national marketing programme as an overlay, with special DMA plans and specific local marketing programmes for each store.

If you are a national package goods company, it may be that, to accomplish your marketing objective of increasing new trial by 10 percent, you need to develop a national marketing programme. However, to help guarantee your success, you will place special marketing and spending emphasis on specific markets that have demonstrated the potential to grow at far greater rates when given local, tailored types of marketing programmes. These local marketing programmes often have their own plans with specific marketing objectives and strategies.

Seasonality Strategies

Strategic decisions must be made about when to advertise or promote your product or store. Here, the seasonality portion of the sales section in your business review becomes useful. Several issues are important. The first is whether there are times of the year when your product category as a whole does significantly better than your company does. If so, why? Can you do something to increase sales during that period when customers of your product category are naturally purchasing at increased rates?

The second issue is whether you are going to advertise and promote all year, during stronger selling periods, or during weaker selling periods. If you have a limited budget, it is recommended that you concentrate only on those times of the year when sales are highest and attempt to capture as many purchases during that period as possible. Often, retail companies utilise in-store promotion strategies, such as bounce-back coupons, during stronger selling periods to entice customers back during down periods, thus using high-volume months to help promote lower-volume months.

Third, you need to decide if you are going to advertise and promote prior to, during, or between peak selling periods. In retail, for example, the holiday seasons are heavy purchasing periods. A strategic decision must be made on whether you are going to advertise earlier than your competitors, throughout the whole selling season, or just during the peak selling weeks. It is often recommended to lead the selling season, because there will be less competitive advertising clutter, and you can build awareness just prior to the heavy shopping period. An alternative strategy that is also successful is to concentrate advertising during the heaviest weeks of the holiday shopping period. Thus, the advertiser can dominate a critical selling period and be visible when it counts most.

Finally, you must consider your resource and production capacity. If your current seasonal sales peaks already have you operating near capacity, you're not going to be able to increase sales much in this period. This is true regardless of your product or service. For a restaurant, it may mean space, tables, and wait staff availability. For a package goods producer, it may be the availability of ingredients. Your marketing expenditures and activities may be used effectively to stimulate demand to accommodate your production or resource limitations.

Spending Strategies

Spending strategies outline how the marketing money will be spent. To achieve your marketing objectives, you need to decide on spending strategies regarding issues such as investment spending for a new product; whether to increase sales of weaker-selling brands, stores, or regions of the country; or whether to attract more customers to your stronger brands or stores. In order to make these decisions, you need to determine spending levels by brand, store, or regions of the country. In most situations you can't increase sales of a weaker-selling brand without making an incremental budget commitment to the brand. We know that one way to increase short-term sales is to place emphasis on a company's strengths. However, there comes a point when strong brands, stores, or markets can't be expected to provide additional growth. Long-term success requires building weaker brands, stores, and sales territories, and this requires some investment spending.

Overall spending should also be addressed. Does your company plan to spend at a percent of sales for marketing and advertising consistent with past years? Or, because of new aggressive sales projections and marketing objectives, do you need to increase marketing spending from, for example, 5 percent of gross sales to 8 percent? The actual spending detail will be highlighted in the budget section of the marketing plan.

Competitive Strategies

There is often need for a competitive strategy. The business review may reveal that a single competitor is almost totally responsible for your company's decline in market share, a new competitor is entering the market, or a single company or group of competitors may have preempted your unique positioning in the marketplace. If this is the case, you will need to develop a competitive marketing strategy in your marketing plan. Competitive strategies vary depending upon the situation. Competitive strategies sometimes use an anti-category strategy, establishing your company as better than all competitors in the category. To achieve this, a company often takes a common, consumer-perceived problem in the industry (such as lack of customer service attention in retail or delayed flights in the airline business), establishes the problem as inherent to the industry, and then tries to set itself apart as better than the competition in this area of concern.

Sometimes competitive strategies focus on one competitor or a group of specific competitors. You may need to reestablish your product attribute dominance relative to a specific competitor, or a competitor may have done a better job of creating a lifestyle image in tune with the heavy-user consumer in your category.

In both of these situations, you might consider developing competitive strategies that require comparison advertising or advertising that counters specific competitive claims. You might also consider a competitive media tactic of advertising within the same time frames and media as your competition. Or you might try to dominate a medium that is lightly used, or perhaps not used at all, by the heavy user of your industry category.

Another common competitive situation occurs when a strong competitor starts doing business in your trading area or in a market you previously dominated. We developed a competitive strategy for a retail client when an aggressive, nationally known competitor announced it was moving into one of our client's important markets. The competitive strategy centered around taking advantage of the fact that our client was already in business and the new competitor wasn't. To implement the strategy, our client ran a half-price sale for two months prior to the opening of the competitor's stores. This was intended to get customers to purchase prior to the anticipated grand opening of the competing stores. The week of the competitor's grand opening, we mailed a promotional piece to consumers in the five-mile trading area surrounding the competitor's store. We continued heavy promotion during the competitor's grand opening by having a grand opening of our own to celebrate the opening of the 240th store in our client's chain of stores.

This competitive plan resulted in our client's stores being up 40 percent during the promotional period and maintaining market share over the long run.

Finally, competitive strategies also include the development of new or improved product, packaging, selling, or merchandising techniques to counter competitive strengths.

Target Market Strategies

Your target market section detailed primary and secondary target markets. You must now discuss the emphasis you will place against the various target markets and how you will market to them based on your marketing objectives, which defined the purchase behavior you intend to gain from the target.

For example, you may decide to target the heavy user through the use of a specific product in your product line that has proven appeal to heavy users or through in-store changes that appeal to heavy users. You may target a secondary target market only through in-store incentives or point-of-purchase promotional techniques, saving all mass media expenditures for the primary target market. Your company may have recently revised your primary target market to include the heavy user who may have shopped your product only as a second choice in the past.

A target market strategy must reflect this change in target market description. This strategy to primarily target the heavy user in all marketing mix decisions affects all subsequent marketing strategies and individual marketing mix tool plans.

Product Strategies

You must make strategic decisions regarding new

products, product line extensions, product improvement, product elimination, and/or whether to build or improve weaker product lines or continue to maximise stronger-selling product lines.

If repeat purchase rates are low and your company's product ranks poorly across product attributes, you must decide how to improve the product in order to meet your marketing objectives. Another area to consider is expanding alternate uses of the product. This is a viable strategy when you have a mature product with a static or limited customer base. An example is the expansion of the use of baking soda as a refrigerator deodoriser. This was a successful marketing strategy designed to meet the marketing objectives of increasing the purchase and usage rates by current customers and providing a reason for new customers to try the product.

The development of new products or new extensions of your existing product line should be addressed if they are necessary to meet marketing objectives. If you are developing new products, you need to establish a new product strategy. Describe in general terms the type of product you will be developing, including the new product's features and attributes. You will also have to address a programme to develop a brand or name for the product.

Again, remember that these should be general strategies that provide overall marketing direction. You should develop a strategy addressing whether you are going to emphasize stronger or weaker product categories/brands in your marketing plan. Selling and emphasizing the products/brands with the greatest potential is particularly viable when growth potential still exists. This strategy can also be used to attract customers through product or store strengths and then cross-sell to weaker-selling categories via promotions or discounts.

Many times a specific target market can also be attracted through the use of loss leaders or a specific strong-selling brand in the product mix. You may have a marketing objective of building new trial among heavy shoe purchasers, women 35 to 44 with children. The problems and opportunities section may point out that women 35 to 44 shop your shoe store not for themselves but for their children. Therefore, your strategy may be to initiate trial by promoting children's shoes to heavy-user women and then cross-sell to the women's shoe department. Other incentives and merchandising techniques could also be created to encourage the purchase of women's shoes once trial is established.

Alternatively, building weaker product categories/ brands is often attempted when it is felt that the company's strengths have been fully exploited. This strategic decision requires more initial money, as it is always more difficult to improve a weakness than to build upon a strength. However, this approach is worthwhile if it provides a company with more products that contribute more equally to profits. This also protects a company from major fluctuations resulting from having only one or two strong-selling products.

Finally, finding more efficient ways to produce the product might also be a viable strategy to help ensure success of a marketing objective if the improved efficiency can permit you to achieve a price advantage. In addition, the improved efficiency might provide greater gross margins, which can help achieve greater profitability or can be invested in stronger marketing programmes.

Naming Strategies

If you are going to introduce a new product or line extension, you will want to provide direction for the naming of these products. Should the new product stand by itself or be under the umbrella of the family name? Should the name target current customers exclusively or current and new customers? If you are going to enter a new channel, you might want to change the name of your product line to appeal to different targets, or you might need a new name for stores carrying your products in discount outlet malls versus regional malls. Strategy Example: Develop a new product name appealing to existing customers first and potential customers second. Rationale: The largest segment of total purchasers is existing customers.

Packaging Strategies

If you are going to develop a packaging plan later in the marketing plan, establish a general direction for your packaging strategy. Here you will need to consider and address the following issues regarding your product's packaging, referring to your problems and opportunities for direction.

1. *Function*: Is your product's packaging serving its primary function of holding or protecting the product?
2. *Value-added*: Does your packaging add value to the product purchase and enhance its use experience for the consumer?
3. *Communication*: Does your packaging stand out in the retail environment compared to competitors? Does it communicate the inherent drama of the product?

A problem identified in the problems and opportunities summaries may point out that the company's packaging makes usage difficult. Therefore, a change in packaging might help achieve the marketing objective of increasing repeat usage and consumption among current customers.

Pricing Strategies

Pricing strategies should also be discussed. One area to address is whether you will use high or low prices relative to your competition, or simply match the competition's price and depend upon service or superior product attributes for a competitive edge. Will you maintain margins with high-price strategies, or will you allow for lower margins and lower prices to develop trial? Also include whether your pricing will be uniform nationally or vary market by market, store by store, or customer by customer. Finally, if you are going to use price to help communicate a positioning, state this intent in this section. Some companies, for example, follow a premium-price strategy to help establish a premium positioning relative to the competition.

Distribution of Product/Penetration or Coverage Strategies

The strategic decisions that must be made in this area for consumer goods and business-to-business firms differ for retailers and service firms. Consumer goods and business-to-business firms must decide in what areas of the country to target their distribution efforts. They also must decide on the type of channels/outlets that will carry their product and on the desired market coverage among the targeted outlet category. Retailers and service firms must strategically decide if marketing objectives can be achieved through existing outlets, whether new stores need to be added in existing markets without cannibalising existing stores, or whether new stores need to be added through entering new markets. If sales per store have not been maximised in low-penetrated markets, one way to build sales is to add new stores in existing markets. This allows for greater leverage of store operation and advertising. However, if sales have been maximised in current markets and the markets have been fully penetrated to the point where additional stores/

products could cannibalise existing sales, then a realistic strategy is to expand to new markets.

Personal Selling/Service/Operation Strategies

You need to determine whether you want to address a structured personal selling programme through this marketing plan. You may want to address basic elements of that sales programme, including whether you will use sales incentives; establish sales goals relative to pure money objectives, a particular product, or target market emphasis in terms of calls made, etc.; and define a sales methodology (e.g., soft sell *versus* hard sell). If you are a retailer, note whether your subsequent selling plan should include specific sales ratios (e.g., develop sales ratio of purchasers *versus* walkers based upon history and future expectations). Like retailers, manufacturers also need to decide whether they are going to establish specific sales ratios. If they choose to do so, a statement such as "establish specific sales ratios (number of prospects that become customers) to monitor the results of the sales force" should be included as a strategy in this section. Additionally, you should consider whether you are going to establish service standards such as the number of days it takes to fill back orders or, for a retailer, the percentage of customers who are greeted as they walk in the door. Finally, if necessary, this section should include a strategy for implementing your marketing department's performance. An example would be to create a marketing liaison between purchasing and marketing to assure the proper inventory levels are maintained during peak promotional times that correspond with heavy media and marketing efforts, as well as historically strong seasonal buying periods.

Promotion/Event Strategies

Promotions should be channeled to meet specific needs and must be incorporated into the overall marketing plan in a disciplined fashion. These promotion strategies will set the areas of emphasis for the specific promotion plan later in the marketing plan, providing direction for the promotional efforts aimed at addressing specific marketing objectives. A retailer may have the marketing objective of increasing the number of units per transaction from the target market by 10 percent over the next twelve months. A marketing strategy to achieve this would be to encourage multiple purchases through promotional incentives. This strategy would then be expanded upon in the promotion section of the marketing plan, but the fact that transaction increases are going to come from multiple-purchase promotional incentives would have been established up front.

Advertising Message Strategies

The marketer needs to provide an overall focus for the advertising and communication. It is important to state up front in your marketing strategy section how you are going to use advertising, to fulfill your marketing objectives. Are you going to develop image advertising and build long-term sales, or will your advertising promote short term sales through a harder-sell, promotional emphasis? Do you plan to vary your advertising message by region? Perhaps you will have both a national advertising programme and a localised, market-by-market programme.

Advertising Media Strategies

The strategies developed in this section should be consistent with the direction established in the product, competitive, and spending marketing strategies. The primary goal in establishing an overall media strategy is to provide direction for the upcoming media plan and to establish geographic and product spending emphasis. You may decide upon a strategy that varies media spending by market or that spends more in markets with greater potential. You may invest in new markets to establish awareness and generate trial. You may consider developing a national media plan or developing both national and local media plans in order to support a dual marketing strategy. You may also address target market reach strategies by identifying how media will be utilised to reach the primary and/ or secondary target market, influencers, etc.

Internet Media Strategies

Your Internet media strategies can center on the Web and E-commerce. The Internet and intranets can be considered as alternative channels of distribution, communication tools, and sales tools. We've found that companies that have a clear direction for the Internet medium for its own purposes will prepare the most effective Internet media strategies.

Merchandising Strategies

A strategy is needed to set the tone for what will be done from a merchandising standpoint. This applies to all non-media communication; for example, in-store signage for retailers, point-of-purchase displays for package goods firms, and personal presentation sales aids such as brochures and sell sheets for business-to-business firms. An opportunity identified under problems and opportunities might tell you that 80 percent of purchase decisions are made in-store. Thus, the marketing strategy in this situation might be to utilise extensive point-of purchase merchandising to affect in-store decision making.

Public Relations Strategies

At this point in your plan development, you should determine if you are going to make public relations part of your marketing plan, as you will need to consider PR opportunities when you develop the other specific tactical tool segments of your plan. For example, you might consider supplementing your overall advertising and promotion communication programme with publicity, or you might use media cosponsors of planned promotional events or a charity "tie-in" to generate publicity. You may decide to develop an extensive public relations programme to take advantage of new product development or ongoing trade show opportunities for your company.

Marketing R & T (Research and Testing) Strategies

Change is often important in generating trial and retrial of a company's product. A disciplined programme to initiate this change is critical. In most businesses there is a need to continually expand and/or refine the company's product offering and marketing in order to continually build incremental sales. This can be accomplished through a planned and disciplined researching and testing programme.

Marketing R & T is the lifeblood for perpetuating the success of your business. It takes time, money, work, planning, and perseverance to research, test, and produce readable results. But it is always worth it!

Research can help define your product's problem(s) and help determine the potential and needs of the target market, optimum pricing, effective advertising messages, and much more. If you plan to conduct primary research, now is the time to establish a research strategy. You may develop a research strategy to solve a specific problem that will help you to build sales and accomplish a marketing objective. Or you may decide to conduct an ongoing awareness, attitude, and behavior tracking study to assist with next year's plan and to provide a benchmark to evaluate the results of current and future marketing plans.

Testing keeps you ahead of the competition and helps you avoid costly mistakes. It can help you develop a new product or marketing activity, make it better, provide evidence of your programme's effectiveness, and eliminate those ideas that aren't going to work before a costly investment has been made. You can test any part of a marketing programme, from a product change and price increase to a new promotion, television commercial, or store format.

Once you have committed to some form of marketing R&T, this Chapter should be used to define what you will be researching and testing-new products, services, merchandising programmes, store layouts, packaging, media strategies, advertising messages, pricing, promotions, etc. Incorporate what you will research and test in the appropriate plan segments later in the marketing plan.

DEVELOP YOUR MARKETING STRATEGY

Developing a marketing strategy is vital for any business. Without one, your efforts to attract customers are likely to be haphazard and inefficient. The focus of your strategy should be making sure that your products and services meet customer needs and developing long-term and profitable relationships with those customers. To achieve this, you will need to create a flexible strategy that can respond to changes in customer perceptions and demand. It may also help you identify whole new markets that you can successfully target.

The purpose of your marketing strategy should be to identify and then communicate the benefits of your business offering to your target market. Once you have created and implemented your strategy, monitor its effectiveness and make any adjustments required to maintain its success.

Marketing Plan

Running a successful business is not like a field of dreams; you can build it but they might not come. Marketing is all about leting people know about the product or service you offer, and persuading them to buy or use it. And for effective marketing you have to let people know about your product or service repeatedly.

To do this, you're going to have to come up with both a marketing strategy and a marketing plan. The marketing strategy is shaped by your overall business goals. It includes a definition of your business, a description of your products or services, a profile of your target users or clients, and defines your company's role in relationship to the competition. The marketing strategy is essentially a document that you use to judge the appropriateness and effectiveness of your specific marketing plans.

To put it another way, your marketing strategy is a summary of your company's products and position in relation to the competition; your sales and marketing plans are the specific actions you're going to undertake to achieve the goals of your marketing strategy.

The marketing plan, then, can be thought of as the practical application of your marketing strategy. It includes details about your business' unique selling proposition, pricing strategy, the sales and distribution plan and your plans for advertising and promotions. So in effect, you can't have a marketing plan without a marketing strategy. But a marketing plan without a marketing strategy is a waste of time. The marketing strategy provides the goals for your marketing plans. It tells you where you want to go from here. The marketing plan is the specific roadmap that's going to get you there.

The first step in developing a marketing plan is to create specific marketing objectives and write them down. What do you want your promotion efforts to do for you? If you're selling herbs, for instance, perhaps you want to increase your monthly sales by 25 percent. If you're a realtor, a good marketing objective might be to get 10 new listings each month. Whatever marketing objective you set, be sure it's realistic; you need to be able to achieve the marketing objective if it's going to motivate you or serve as a good benchmark to evaluate your success.

Once you set up your marketing plan, remember that it needs to be an organic, living document, not something you put into a nice folder and file somewhere and never look at again. Take fifteen minutes every day to review your goals and specific activities; what did you do that particular day to help you achieve the marketing objectives you've set?

What do you need to do tomorrow? Too often we make plans or list objectives and then get so enmeshed in all the things we have to do to run our businesses that we shunt them aside. Taking fifteen minutes a day to review your marketing objectives, marketing plan, and marketing activities goes a long way towards helping you stay focused and on track and market your products or services effectively.

TOWARDS A SUCCESSFUL MARKETING STRATEGY

One of the key elements of a successful marketing strategy is the acknowledgement that your existing and potential customers will fall into particular groups or segments, characterised by their "needs". Identifying these groups and their needs through market research, and then addressing them more successfully than your competitors, should be the focus of your strategy.

You can then create a marketing strategy that makes the most of your strengths and matches them to the needs of the customers you want to target. For example, if a particular group of customers is looking for quality first and foremost, then any marketing activity aimed at them should draw attention to the high quality service you can provide.

Once this has been completed, decide on the best marketing activity that will ensure your target market know about the products or services you offer, and why they meet their needs. This could be achieved through various forms of advertising, exhibitions, public relations initiatives, Internet activity and by creating an effective "point of sale" strategy if you rely on others to actually sell your products. Limit your activities to those methods you think will work best, avoiding spreading your budget too thinly.

A key element often overlooked is that of monitoring and evaluating how effective your strategy has been. This control element not only helps you see how the strategy is performing in practice, it can also help inform your future marketing strategy. A simple device is to ask each new customer how they heard about your business.

Once you have decided on your marketing strategy, draw up a marketing plan to set out how you plan to execute and evaluate the success of that strategy. The plan should be constantly reviewed so it can respond quickly to changes in customer needs and attitudes in your industry, and in the broader economic climate.

Know your Strengths and Weaknesses

Your strategy must take account of how your business' strengths and weaknesses will affect your marketing.

Begin your marketing strategy document with an honest and rigorous SWOT (Strengths, Weaknesses, Opportunities, and Threats) analysis, looking at your strengths, weaknesses, opportunities and threats. It is a good idea to conduct some market research on your existing customers at this point, as it will help you to build a more honest picture of your reputation in the marketplace.

Strengths could include:

— Personal and flexible customer service.

— Special features or benefits that your product offers.

— Specialist knowledge or skills.

Weaknesses could include:

— Limited financial resources.

— Lack of an established reputation.

— Inefficient accounting systems.

Opportunities could include:

— Increased demand from a particular market sector.

— Using the Internet to reach new markets.

— New technologies that allow you to improve product quality.

Threats could include:

— The emergence of a new competitor.

— More sophisticated, attractive or cheaper versions of your product or service.

— New legislation increasing your costs.

— A downturn in the economy, reducing overall demand.

Writing Your Marketing Strategies

Make sure to focus on one single idea at a time when writing your strategies. The strategies should be very descriptive and focus on how you are going to utilise a particular tool, such as promotions or packaging, to achieve the marketing objectives. Following each strategy should be a brief rationale drawing information from the business review, problems and opportunities, opportunities, target market and marketing objectives, and market positioning sections to support the strategy.

When you are writing a business plan, the Marketing and Sales Strategies section is an important part of your formal business plan. This part of writing a business plan essentially involves developing a marketing and sales strategy for your business.

Marketing and Sales Strategies Section

When you are writing a business plan, the Marketing and Sales Strategies section should include:

- How you will promote your business.
- How you will get your product or service to your customers.
- The costs to promote and distribute you products or services.
- How you will measure the effectiveness of the methods you plan to use.

Writing a Marketing Plan

Once you've completed the Market Analysis section of your business plan, you'll know more about your customers, your competition and your company. That information should make writing the Sales and Marketing Strategy section of your business plan all the easier.

Depending on how detailed your marketing plan is, you may include the marketing plan in its entirety while you are writing this section of your business plan or you may just want to include highlights of your marketing plan. If you are writing a business plan and only including highlights of your marketing plan, you'll want to make sure that the marketing plan is complete in case an investor requests the entire document.

Those who are considering lending your small business money or investing will want to know how you intend to reach your target market and attain the market share you feel you can attain, which you've already discussed in the Market Analysis section of your business plan. Your marketing plan will help them understand that.

4

BRAND POSITIONING

Brand positioning is probably one of the most confused concepts in the world of business today. A brand positioning is not a clever advertising idea, a cool tag line, a slick logo, a graphic standards manual, or a website. While these and other elements combine to contribute to your brand positioning, they are not the foundation. The result of a brand positioning is the thought triggered in the mind of the consumer when he or she hears and/ or sees your name. A brand is far more than advertising. It's the identity an organisation has internally and externally. It represents the values, the personality, and the experience that people associate with the company, product, or service.

A brand provides a point of difference—a reason to choose your company, product, or service over the competition. This is increasingly important in today's parity-product environment. Brands help companies command a premium price because of the added value associated with brands. Brands promise quality; they boost earnings and cushion downturns in the economy. Most important, not only does a strong brand help customers understand your company, but it also imparts a sense of mission within the company. A good brand positioning provides guidelines for every action from product development.

A brand image of your company, product, or service evolves whether you are directly involved in shaping the process or not. Think of French people. Think of the little redheaded boy, the blonde cheerleader, Irish people, New Orleans, Nike, IBM, Intel, Starbucks, Ford, Firestone tires. Images immediately come to mind that describe each of these examples. Everything gets branded, whether by a disciplined process or by people's perceptions over time. It's a critical function of the marketing plan to help shape those perceptions.

Brand positioning then is a process of establishing and managing the images, perceptions, and associations that the consumer applies to your product based on the values and beliefs associated with your product. These are managed through application of the brand positioning elements, consistent with the product's positioning, in all target market communication relating to your company, product, or service. The more effective you are in your brand positioning, the greater the value your brand holds for you. The value of the brand, above and beyond the cumulative physical attributes of the product itself, represents brand equity.

Developing a brand and building equity in that brand are the broad components of the branding process. In this process, you have one goal for the brand: to generate consistent purchase behaviour among a target base. In other words, you seek to build and maintain brand loyalty. Consumers also have sweet spots. When your marketing or communications idea hits that sweet spot, your sales will go flying. The sweet spot is the place in the target person's mind where you make the connection between a consumer's insight and the product or brand insight. You might think of it this way:

Consumer Insight + Product Insight = Sweet Spot

What we are saying here is that you must define your customers or potential consumers by the way they think of themselves and how they look at life. You must look at your product not for what you believe it offers but for what they expect and receive from your type of product. Another way you can look at the sweet spot concept is by combining a rational benefit via product insight and an emotional need via consumer insight—a strong combination for a strong brand positioning. While the sweet spot concept is one way of describing brand positioning, another way is for you to take the following quiz and answer each question.

1. Who was the first person to fly solo across the North Atlantic Ocean? Who was the second?
2. Who was the first person to walk on the moon? Who was the second?
3. What is the highest mountain in the world? What is the second highest?
4. Who is first in copiers? Who is second?

If you are like most people, you could answer the" first" questions correctly for one through three, but have a difficult time answering who was second. And, as for question number four, most answer "Who is first in copiers?" with Xerox, which is wrong. The correct answer is Canon Copiers, which has been number one for almost two decades. However, Xerox is still usually perceived as first in copiers. And that's the point. Securing a meaningful place in the minds of the target market, such as first, sets the product apart from all the others and causes it to be remembered. The lesson here is that, like a memory bank, people's minds have slots or positions, with one position or slot for each piece of information they have chosen to keep. You want your product to own that one position. Successful positioning is the art of sacrifice. You can't be all things to all people and create an effective positioning. Positioning is about the one main thing that your company, product, or service stands for. The question is how to develop this positioning equity in the minds of people within our target market. Let's begin with a formal definition of positioning.

IMPORTANCE OF POSITIONING

Positioning establishes the desired perception of your product within the target market relative to the competition. If there is no real or direct competition (such as for some nonprofit organisations), the organisation still needs a point of reference in order for the target market to understand and remember what is being communicated. In the case of the competitive marketplace, a positioning positively differentiates the product from the competition. Remember, positioning is used to differentiate your product to a specific target market, not to the whole world.

No matter what you are marketing, salient positioning is necessary. Positioning is the basis for all of your communications—naming, advertising, promotions, packaging, sales force, merchandising, and publicity. By having one meaningful, targeted positioning as a guide for all communications, you will convey a consistent image. By conveying a common positioning, each vehicle of communication will reinforce the others for a cumulative effect, maximising the rectums of your marketing investment. Accordingly, everything you do from a marketing perspective must reinforce one positioning. Otherwise, you will undermine your marketing efforts and confuse the target group as well.

Further, because everything you do should reflect one positioning, the positioning must be correct, or your marketing activities will be ineffective. Worse yet, incorrect positioning could even destroy a successful product. You must look for a positioning that not only is right for your product now but that will also be adaptable years into the future for both the marketplace and the product.

POSITIONING CONSIDERATIONS

In order to arrive at a successful long-term positioning, you must take into consideration these factors:

- The inherent drama of the product you are selling.
- The needs and wants of the target markets.
- The competition.

The business review and the problems and opportunities you have completed, long with the target market determination and marketing objectives you develops are key to arriving at the right positioning. You must understand the strengths and weaknesses of your product versus that of the competition. Where is your product comparable to the competition and where is it different? Where is it unique? Most important, what do these competitive differences, if any, mean to the target market? If the positioning reflects a difference that your product cannot deliver or that is not important to the target group, your positioning will not be successful. Even if your product possesses a meaningful difference, your positioning will not be effective if the target group does not perceive it as meaningfully different. The key point is that, as you develop your product positioning, you must deal with the target group's perception of the competing products, even if it is not altogether accurate, because they are the buyers, and consequently, their perception is truth.

Further, the odds of arriving at a successful positioning increase dramatically when you have done market research of the potential target market. Primary research will help identify key users/purchasers and meaningful product attributes. Also, quantitative research will show how the primary market perceives these important attributes relative to the competition. Even without primary market research, if you have diligently employed the disciplined marketing plan process, you should have a good start in developing a positioning that communicates effectively to the target market.

Everything in a marketing plan evolves from the target market and how you strategically meet the needs of the target market with your product. Therefore, no matter how you position your product, the target market must be central to the positioning. As you consider various positioning alternatives, let the problems and opportunities of the business review be the basis, the target market be the focal point, and the marketing objectives provide direction.

DEVELOP YOUR OWN POSITIONING

A positioning statement answers one or more of the following questions:

1. Who is it for? (Mountain Dew is for young Extreme-sport risk takers.)
2. What does it do? (AAA is a travel membership organisation that provides peace of mind.)
3. How is it different? (Eastpak backpacks last longer.)

A company, product, or service organisation can be different across three dimensions. There can be a product difference, a customer service difference, or an experience difference. Intel, with the "chip inside," has positioned around a product difference. In today's world of product and service parity, many companies are working hard to provide an experiential difference.

The following steps to help you position your product:

1. Use the three positioning methods of matching, mapping, and emotional relationship to thoroughly

understand how your product relates to the target market and the competition. In order to fully utilise these three approaches, you must have a thorough understanding of the business review and, particularly, of the problems and opportunities summary of your marketing background section.

2. Prepare a positioning strategy.
3. Review potential positioning executions and decide which is best for implementing the positioning strategy for your product.

Positioning by Matching

Simply stated, this positioning method matches your product's inherent and unique benefits or competitive advantage to the characteristics and needs/wants of the target market.

Task 1

Analyse your product versus the competition:

A good place to start the matching method is with an analysis of your product and your competition. The competition could be one major competitor, a number of key competitors, a specific business category, or a number of key business categories. In the positioning of an off-price menswear retailer, it was determined that specific competition varied by geographic market, but the competitive business categories remained the same in all markets—departmental stores, speciality men's clothing stores, and off-price/discount stores.

Task 2

Identify product differences versus the competition:

Next, write down the key positive and negative differences of your product versus those of the competition relative to your primary target market. These differences should be listed as they relate to key elements of the marketing mix that are appropriate to what you are selling.

Sometimes a difference that is seemingly negative can become a positive. A small retailer with limited square footage and, thereby, limited variety of product offering can create a positioning of speciality selection and personal attention.

For each area, ask yourself, "How is my product different and how is it better?" Is your product different through product superiority, innovation, or size-number of customers, volume of goods sold, number of outlets? Whenever possible, use quantitative research for objectivity.

Task 3

List your key target market:

Insert your key target market on the top right side of the same worksheet.

Task 4

List key target market characteristics:

Now, list the characteristics of your target market in terms of wants and needs on the right side of the worksheet. With or without research, ask yourself the following questions, listing brief answers below each question:

- What is the target market really purchasing? Is the product to be used by itself or in conjunction with a number of products? For what purpose is the target using the product?
- Where is the target market purchasing/using it—by geography (e.g., in sunny, very warm climates) and/ or by place (in the home, car, etc.)?

— When is the target market using it-time of the year, month, week, day, during or after work?
— Why is the target market purchasing and/ or using the product or why are they purchasing from one store over another? Is it because of a particular feature? Is it a convenient location or greater selection? Does the product save time or money?
— How is it purchased/used? Is it purchased/used alone or with other people? Is it a frequent or infrequent purchase? How is it used?
— How is the target changing? Is the market changing by demographics, lifestyle or size? How are purchasing/ usage habits of the product changing?

Task 5

Match your product's characteristics to the target market's needs/ wants:

Having listed the differences of your product and the key needs/wants of the target market, try to match what is unique about your product to the meaningful needs and wants of the target market. Based on the listing of the competitive differences, it would appear that this fabric retailer has a competitive advantage by offering an abundance of fabric-related merchandise in larger, better-designed stores. The merchandise selection appears superior not only in the amount but also in the variety of merchandise offered to complete a sewing project, as well as related crafting and home decorating projects. This retailer could be viewed as a leader with an established reputation offering a variety of quality merchandise, though not at the lowest prices or greatest values.

The target market, on the other hand, is a mix of both practically and recreationally motivated sewers who want a large selection of all types of fabric-related merchandise that is very competitively priced and is a real value. This retailer definitely has the desired selection and quality but not necessarily the lower prices and value. The target also wants all of the required merchandise under one roof in order to enjoy a fun and rewarding shopping experience, as well as to fulfil the needs for both practically and recreationally motivated projects. Further, the listing indicates changes occurring within the target market. It appears that people with sew have less time or need to sew regularly, are creating fewer garments, and are becoming more recreationally oriented, with interest growing in craft and home decorating projects.

There appears to be a number of competitive advantages that are important for meeting the target's needs, including wide variety, quality, fissionability, growing selection, and larger stores. These advantages would appear to match the target's growing desire for a fabric store with a large and complete offering of sewing, craft, and home decorating merchandise.

By matching the key differences to the key target market needs/ wants of the positioning listings, you could arrive at the following positioning statement for this fabric retail chain: "Each store provides everything a woman needs to fulfil fabricrelated sewing, crafting, and home decorating expectations." After you have prepared your positioning worksheet, draw lines from the major competitive positive differences to the paralleling want/ need characteristics of the target market. Ask yourself again what really is important to the target market in terms of how your product is different and better. Based on this, eliminate lines until you have the two or three most meaningful potential positioning connections between product and target market.

In some cases you might combine two product differences or advantages to fill an important want. If you were a retailer, you might combine the attributes of brand-name products and very competitive prices to arrive at a value positioning, which ties to an important consumer desire.

In some situations you will draw lines between product and target market characteristics and find that a most important consumer need/want is not being fulfilled by your product or the competition. Going to the other extreme, you might find that all of the competing products fulfil the target's need/want, but no one competitor, including your product, has claimed it as a reason for being. Or, it might be that there are changing needs that are not being met and evolving needs that will provide positioning opportunities.

The competitors are other regional accounting firms. However, this accounting firm does more than just measure financial strength; it works across a client's business, with a concentration on how the interrelated parts affect the whole. In order to do this, the firm had to develop centres of excellence throughout a wide number of departments, including personnel, technology, strategic planning, and various areas of financial expertise. Research showed that members of the target market found it difficult to determine the value of one accounting firm over another and thus were looking for a firm with which they could build a long-term relationship over time and that would get to know their business. Accounting clients also wanted more than just reporting; they wanted solutions that would be actionable.

The firm had a proven staff of regionally known experts heading up the individual departments. It also had strong testimonials citing proven results from companies that used the firm's approach of attacking the many parts to provide for a better system bottom line. The businesses were becoming more in tune with the fact that a combination of factors affect profitability. If you fix the accounting system but don't have the right technology or staff, you won't solve the overall problem. The target market also demonstrates repeatedly the desire for one source to bring tangible ways to increase the overall bottom-line performance of the company.

The positioning became systemic solutions resulting in improved profits. The new positioning led to many new business wins. Probably just as important, the firm felt the positioning significantly helped its recruiting. The company attracted better, more aggressive candidates who wanted to be part of-everything the new positioning communicated versus the traditional, conservative images stereotypical of accounting firms.

Positioning by Mapping

This approach is a practical application of mapping methodology based on multidimensional models. Although the mapping approach is theoretical in origin, we actively use it in the positioning of our clients' products and services. Using this approach, you map out visually what is important to your target market in terms of key product attributes. The competition's products, along with your own, are then ranked on these attributes. This type of mapping is extremely useful in positioning a product and, again, is most effective when based on quantitative research that is representative of the marketplace. Your preconceived notions about what the target market thinks can differ dramatically from what quantifiable research reports.

However, if you do not have market research, it is still helpful to use this method when positioning to help sort out what you believe is important to the target market. Further, this positioning approach will help you to more clearly evaluate how your product and your key competition are perceived on each attribute. Because this mapping method is somewhat involved and you will most likely not have research to assist you, read through the three steps before beginning the actual mapping process.

Task 1

List product attributes by importance:

In the retail category, the most important attribute to the consumer might be quality, followed by selection, price, service, and fashion, with location listed at the bottom. In business-tobusiness, reliable delivery might be ranked most important, followed by product consistency, quality, price, and favorable reputation, with knowledgeable sales force being least important.

Task 2

Rate your product and competitors' products for each attribute:

Once you have listed the key target market attributes, rate each competitor from best to worst for each attribute. For each rating, place the initial of each key competitor, including your product, on the line of each attribute ranking. Make a master listing of these keys under company /product/store. If quantitative research is not available before you begin mapping, it's a good idea to gather a number of people knowledgeable about your product category and have each one of them list the most important attributes. Next, as objectively as possible, have them independently assign a number from 1 to 10 (10 being most important and 1 least important) for each attribute. Take an average of these estimates for each ranking. Based on each composite estimate, ranks order the attributes. After ranking attribute importance, ask the participants to agree on the top three to five market competitors, including your product. Then have each of them independently assign a rating of 1 to 10 for each competitor on each attribute, with 10 being best. Average the ratings for each competitor and insert a rating for each competitor, by initial, in line with each attribute ranking. In your plotting of the competitive market, you might have great disparity between competitors on one attribute and no differences on another. Ideally, you want your product ranked the best versus the competition on all attributes, but particularly on those that are most important to the consumer.

Task 3

Visualise desired position on the map for your product:

Once your positioning map is complete, review how your product ranks on the more important attributes relative to the competition. Next, visualise where you want your product positioned on the map based on what the consumer wants and what your product can provide relative to strengths and weaknesses of the competition.

POSITIONING BY EMOTIONAL RELATIONSHIP

All positioning efforts seek to establish a connection between product and target market. But the emphasis can differ dramatically. Attribute positioning, which is the basis for the mapping method, focuses on the target's rating of the product relative to the competition; it focuses more on attributes like value, quality, or convenience. Emotional relationship positioning emphasizes the feelings of the target market: their feelings about the product, about themselves or about others, toward the company's personality, and about the meaning of the product in their lives.

This more "emotional" approach offers a number of advantages:

- Once a relationship is established, it is harder for competitors to attack than specific product attributes.

— You can maintain the relationship despite radical changes in technology or product features.

There are also some disadvantages to this approach:

— If your product has a unique advantage (for example, a patented process), this approach may not focus enough on the product.

— If you cannot afford the media expenses to establish and defend this position, a larger, better-funded competitor can steal it from you.

— You must be able to deliver on the emotional promise. If you promise "friendly" and deliver "indifferent," you will make matters worse.

In many business categories, the marketing battleground has already seen some movement from rational benefits to emotional relationships. The reason? The consumer now faces a bewildering array of product choices. Unique product features or technical breakthroughs are quickly duplicated. The result is that the consumer does not have the time or energy to know everything necessary to make the right choice. He or she needs a simple relationship with a company that can be counted on over time to be a good choice.

The value of an emotional relationship with the company is even greater when there is high emotional involvement in product selection (perfume).

— The competitive frame is saturated and complex (soft drinks).

— The degree of personal, financial, or emotional risk is great (cars).

— The business category is perceived as a commodity (sugar).

Having an emotional relationship with a company or product is like having a relationship with another person.

- How does this relationship make me feel about myself?
- What will other people think of me?
- What key emotional needs does this relationship meet?
- What personality characteristics can I count on over time and across product experiences?
- What values does this company stand for?

Many of these emotional questions are subconscious and irrational. They may even sound silly when stated out loud. Building an emotional relationship starts with the consumer rather than with your company or product. The goal is to build on consumers' feelings, perceptions, and emotional needs. You will have to live in the consumer's hidden emotional world. Emotional relationship marketing requires the use of fairly sophisticated qualitative research techniques, the ability to listen "behind" or "below" what consumers are saying, and the ability to create a wide range of positioning hypotheses to test. Before you undertake emotional relationship positioning, you may want to seek the assistance of a marketing communications firm, an advertising agency, or a marketing research firm with proven experience in this area.

If you explore how to do relationship positioning, you may find it helpful to look at the experience of one of our clients.

Build an Emotional Relationship with the Consumer

Task 1

Develop an individual profile of your highest-opportunity consumer:

This individual profile contains things like demographics, lifestyle, values, emotional needs, life experiences, philosophies, hobbies, and interests of the heavy purchaser. This profile is then contrasted with that of the person who is the lowest opportunity consumer or the light purchaser. This contrast will often point to the key underlying motivator.

Task 2

Brainstorm for motivators:

Brainstorm with your staff or people knowledgeable about the product to develop a wide. range of underlying, feelinggenerated motivators to test with consumers. It is even valuable to include motivators that you know are wrong in order to get clearer feedback that points you in the right direction.

Task 3

Rank the motivator choices with target consumers:

For example, DeanCare focus group members were shown positioning both in the form of written boards and as tape-recorded patient statements. Participants then ranked fifth most favourite and least favourite statements. You should plan to do a minimum of two different focus groups.

Task 4

Identify the consumer's primary emotional motivator(s):

Motivations can differ significantly depending on the purchasing occasion, the stage of your life, or the role the product plays in your life.

Task 5

Validate qualitative analysis with quantitative survey results:

If at all possible, use survey research to test several different positioning to verify the results of the focus groups regarding the appeal of the key motivator relative to the size of the market. This will prevent you from selecting a key motivator that is very strong but that is significant only for a very small group of people.

Task 6

Use the strongest motivator for positioning strategy:

This will establish a relationship with your target person and also establish a core brand personality for your company or product.

PREPARE A POSITIONING STRATEGY

Having gone through the matching, mapping, and emotional relationship methods with your product, you should now have some direction or thoughts on how you want your product to be perceived as meaningfully different from the competition by the target market. With this, you are ready to write alternative positioning strategies. It is wise to write more than one positioning strategy in order to make a comparison of strategies and evaluate which positioning best reflects your product elative to the competition and fulfils the needs/wants of the target market. Your alternative positioning statements should vary by the degree of emphasis placed on the product advantage, the competition's weaknesses, and the target market benefit. The key word is focus when writing a positioning statement. Rather than keeping it simple and straightforward, the tendency is to write a positioning statement that reads like a litany. The shorter and more to the point, the better the positioning strategy. A succinct positioning will provide clear and specific direction for the employment of the tactical marketing mix tools. For this reason, choose each word that you use in your positioning statement thoughtfully.

The following is a three-step process that you might want to use to prepare your positioning strategy.

1. Look for meaningful differences.
2. Prepare alternative positioning strategies that vary by degree of emphasis:
   - Product advantages.
   - Target market benefit.
   - Competitor weaknesses.
3. Decide on a final strategy that has focus.

Select a Positioning Execution

Having decided on a positioning strategy, the final step is to develop an execution for that strategy. This step is particularly important to the communication of that strategy across all of the tactical marketing mix tools.

Positioning by Product Difference

Ask yourself: What is meaningfully different about what my company is selling? Do I have a unique product feature? Pillsbury took a commodity productflour and put a recipe inside the sack to make it different from the competition, calling it "the Idea Flour." Another example of using a product difference as a feature is Famous Fixtures, a manufacturer and installer of store fixtures that sells to retail store chains. It positioned itself as having actual retail experience, because its own parent company is a retailer.

Positioning by Key Attribute/Benefit

Ask yourself: What benefit does my product offer that the target market will consider meaningful? Many times the image you position outside your organisation can have a major positive effect on those employed within the organisation to deliver on that positioning.

The meaningful attributes to the purchaser and user vary by product and service. In the retail area, the key consumer attributes are usually quality, selection, price, service, and location. Depending on the concept you are retailing, the order of the attributes will change according to their importance to your target market. For example, quality and price are important not just for retailers but to the positioning of many other products and services as well. A key point to remember is that the two attributes of quality and price very often translate into a third important attribute: value. However, value can be driven by the combination of many other different attributes as well, including selection, service, and durability. Value is a good competitive image to own if you can first establish it and then hold it.

Positioning by the Users of Your Product

By going right to the users/purchasers of your product, your positioning will become more salient to the target market, creating an image among this group that the place, product, or service is especially for them.

5

MARKETING COMMUNICATION

In most situations, a person must have a positive attitude toward the product before the initial action can take place. This could involve a long-term attitude development process, such as in the buying process of a new automobile, or low attitude involvement, such as that leading to an impulse purchase of a pack of gum at the checkout register, For example, even if the name of the gum is unfamiliar to you, you form an attitude toward the gum, however fleeting, from what is communicated via the brand name, how the gum is packaged! displayed, and perhaps the price. Your attitude toward a product could also be formed by some previous action or experience, such as sampling, but not buying, a product or calling for a brochure. Or, it may be that you had a positive attitude toward a product and purchased it, but after a bad experience with it, you subsequently formed a negative attitude and never purchased that product again.

MARKETING COMMUNICATION PROCESS ON SALES

Now that you have an understanding of the Four A's communication and target-market behaviour\process, we will explain how this process interfaces with other plan elements and the ultimate goal of generating sales. In this process, the cumulative effect of the specific awareness and attitude generated from each tactical tool fulfils the overall marketing plan communication goals. The overall marketing plan communication delivers the positioning via the marketing strategies that fulfil the marketing objectives of target market behaviour that will, in turn, fulfil the sales objectives.

Marketing Objectives and Communication

By now you should have arrived at a sales objective and quantified the target market segment(s) that will deliver the sales. Also, you should have quantified the behaviour required by the target market in your marketing objectives. What we will explain next is how to arrive at the purchase intent and required marketing plan awareness and attitude communication needed to generate the required behaviour. We will then detail a methodology to arrive at the individual tactical tool awareness and attitude communication needed to fulfil the marketing plan communication goals.

Development of Purchase Intent and Communication Goals

The four tasks to follow for developing and fulfilling the purchase intent and the marketing communication goals via tactical tool communication are:

1. Review awareness, attitude, and behaviour experiences for your product, the competition, the category, and related categories as outlined in your business review.
2. Review the previously established target market behaviour that has been quantified in your marketing objectives for both purchasers and nonpurchasers, as well as the marketing position and strategies.

3. Determine the overall marketing plan communication goals.
   - *(a)* Determine the attitude required by your target market to deliver the purchase intent needed to fulfil the marketing objectives.
   - *(b)* Determine the awareness levels necessary to positively affect target market attitude as required to achieve the predetermined purchase intent.
4. Set specific awareness and attitude value goals for each tactical tool that will fulfil the overall marketing communication goals.

Communication Goals Application

Now that you have a basic understanding of the relationship between communication and behaviour and have been exposed to the four steps involved in locking the tactical tools to the marketing communication goals, we will describe the application of each task. Then, we will review the limitations and complexity of this process as it relates to the unique communication control challenges and inherent problems of your product and category. In addition, we will point out the difficulties in the measurement of the communication contribution of each of the tactical tools in the marketing mix.

Task 1

Review Awareness, Attitude, and Action/Behaviour Experiences for Your Product, the Competition, the Category, and Related Categories Literally all small, medium, and even large businesses lack much of the described information needed to apply the ideal communication goals method. Hopefully, you have gathered much data in your business review that you can use as a basis in the application of this method.

Specifically, look for information that will provide insight as to each tactical tool's ability to deliver awareness and positive attitude to generate behaviour and/ or make the sale. You would like to have some indication as to what percentage of the target market is aware of your product and holds key attitudes toward your product, such as best quality, leadership, and so on, and how these communication factors relate to the percentage of your target market that purchases the product.

If possible, you would like to know the awareness, attitude, and behaviour of both customers and noncustomers in your target market, because you will find that the relationship between communication and behaviour will vary dramatically between purchasers and nonpurchasers

Understand your own product history:

Begin your review of awareness, attitude, and behaviour data with your own product, store, or service. You should have uncovered some of this communication and behavioural data in the preparation of your business review. Next, review your business data for cause-and-effect relationship. For example, when a manufacturer secures display placements in 25 percent or more of the retail outlets in his services area, he sees an increase in sales of 30-50 percent. Or, when a business-to-business manufacturer receives placement of a feature article in a major industry trade publication, he generally sees an increase of 60-70 percent in inquiries. With this same manufacturer, over half of the inquiries each year can be tracked back to those trade shows at which there was a booth. Or, when a retailer runs a test in which only the execution of one tool was changed (promotion tool changed from composing to sampling), sales increase 15 percent in test markets as compared to the control markets where no change was made.

If you have not been measuring and recording the effectiveness of the various tools or testing their effectiveness, it is something you will want to include in next year's plan. While observations like those in the preceding examples measure cause and effect but do not answer the awareness and attitude questions, you can use this basic information to help estimate what percentage of the target market's unaided awareness and attitude caused the behaviour. For example, if running twice the number of ads in a given period increased calls by 50 percent, the inference would be that there was a minimum of 50 percent increase in awareness created by doubling the number of ads. These types of inferences are far from empirical research, but they do provide some direction.

Implement primary research:

While being able to relate cause and effect is a start to learning, it is necessary to do primary research to more accurately determine the awareness, attitude, and behaviour levels of purchasers and nonpurchasers for your product and that of the competition. In most cases, the awareness, attitude, and behaviour data derived from the survey research will be cumulative in nature and will not provide specific information for each tool. However, by applying the cause-and effect information you have collected by each tool, you might be able to learn directionally about each tool's effect on awareness and attitude. For example, let's say that your primary research indicated a 40 percent unaided awareness for your product among the target market and that, by your applying only three tactical marketing mix tools—personal selling, merchandising (product brochure for follow-up), and public relations—it was shown that 70 percent of your noncustomer inquiries came from editorial messages in trade publications, the direct result of your public relations programmes. If this were the case, you could surmise that 70 percent of the total awareness came from the public relations tool and, therefore, could allocate 28 points (.70 x .40 = 28 points) of current awareness to this tool. This is a very rough approach to allocation, but again, it demonstrates how you can use the interpolation of cause-and-effect data with research derived awareness, attitude, and behaviour data to arrive at an individual communication value for a tactical tool.

Many times companies use primary research to measure the effectiveness of specific vehicles or tactical tools. For example, with our client Famous Footwear we found that, for a specific promotion, 24 percent of the customers came to the stores because of an FSI (free-standing insert), while only 4 percent of customers came because of a newspaper ad. While primary research will provide much insight in terms of awareness, attitude, and behaviour information for your product and the competition, you can also learn more about cause and effect by reviewing the tactical activity of your competition and their expenditures relative to specific tools and total marketing budget. This is usually difficult information to uncover, but hopefully in your competitive review in the business review you have arrived at some cause-and-effect information that you can relate to specific tactical tools.

Review secondary sources:

In addition to doing primary research to help you determine value data for your marketing plan communication goals and individual tactical tools, you should review industry and trade association publications for research studies that have been implemented. You should also review studies done within specific disciplines, such as Advertising Age for the advertising message, Inside Media for the advertising media, and Promo for the promotion tool. You can review some of the publications oriented to the academic world, such as the Journal of Consumer Research and Journal of Advertising Research, for insight into the impact of tactical tools, both individually and cumulatively, on various types and levels of awareness, attitude, and behaviour.

From this type of review you will arrive at specific quantitative information that you can apply when determining your marketing plan communication goals and values for each tool. However, in most situations, your review of this type of information will lead only to broad, directional inferences that you can apply in the "value method." This review will also clearly point out what you know, what you don't know, and what you need to know about the relationship between communication and behaviour relative to your product. Also you will learn that most of the information you will apply is more subjective than objective. In fact, before developing the goals method, we went through a mental allocation process to determine what awareness and attitude thresholds were required for the marketing communication goals and each tactical tool. This method, while far from perfect, merely improves the chance for success in locking the marketing plan elements together most efficiently and effectively by providing a framework.

Task 2

Review marketing objectives, positioning, and strategies:

In order to set the tactical tool values and then lock them to the marketing plan communication goals, you must understand the requirements of the marketing behaviour objectives, and the direction provided by the position and marketing strategies.

Marketing objectives:

First review the specific behaviour required in terms of retention of current purchasers, trial by new purchasers, and the amount of annual product purchased by both current and new purchasers. Ask yourself this question: Where is the greatest emphasis in terms of required behaviour versus the previous years? Is the primary emphasis on retention or trial? For example, if the emphasis is on trial and new customers, you will need greater awareness among nonpurchasers for your marketing plan communication goal, and accordingly, you will potentially require more support from specific tactical tools designed to generate greater exposure for your product, such as advertising media and publicity.

What is the total amount of product to be purchased by the current and new customers as called for in the marketing objectives? If the objectives call for substantial increases in the amount of purchases by small numbers of target companies or persons, you might consider greater support from tactical tools that are close to the point of purchase, such as personal selling or merchandising through store displays that encourage impulse purchase, and "loading" types of promotions (e.g., buy two, get one free).

What are the expectation levels for repeat buying and building loyalty among new customers that have tried the product? In this case, product performance and personal service could be tools used for more support.

Marketing strategies:

Remember, each of the marketing strategies will provide direction indicating which tactical tools will be used and how they should be used to help communicate the position in terms of building awareness, presenting a positive attitude, and, in turn, fulfilling the marketing objectives.

First, review how the marketing strategies might have changed from the previous years. For example, does the distribution strategy call for a greater ACV (all commodity volume) distribution or store penetration in existing markets, which will have lead to greater awareness? Was there a change in the pricing strategy from premium to commodity pricing? While the actual pricing of the product will usually have minimal, if any, effect on awareness, it will affect the target market's attitude toward this product.

Further, review each strategy in terms of awareness and attitude delivery and attempt to determine if there was any change from the previous year in importance relative to the use of other strategies in delivering the overall marketing plan communication goals. For example, was there a shift in importance from personal selling to advertising media in building awareness and positive attitude toward the product? Note these changes when identifying what communication value you expect from each tactical tool.

Task 3

Purchase Intent:

Now that you have a greater (but never complete) understanding of the relationship between communication and behaviour for your product and category and you have reviewed the marketing objectives, positioning, and marketing strategies, you must next make some product purchase estimates. You should first attempt to estimate what percent of the target market purchasers believe they will definitely continue as purchasing customers and what percent of the target nonpurchasers believe they will definitely become new purchasers.

Sometimes your research database will indicate what percent of target purchasers and target nonpurchasers believe they will definitely purchase your product. If you do not have this type of information—which will be the case for most products—you should make this estimate based on the information reviewed in Task 1. To help you make this estimate, you can break down each target segment from "definitely will not purchase" to "possibly will not purchase," "possibly will purchase," and finally, "definitely will purchase." A starting point for goal estimation is provided just after the forthcoming discussion of attitude and awareness.

Attitude and awareness:

Next, from your review of the data in Task I, determine what percent of the target purchasers and non-purchasers will have to hold a specific attitude toward the product in order to arrive at the specific percentage of each base that definitely will purchase. Then, determine what percent of the target customers and target non-customers must have unaided awareness of the product in order to affect the intended attitude and the predetermined purchase intent. "First mention" or "top-of mind" awareness can be used as a goal in place of total unaided awareness; aided awareness should not be used as a goal because it is not a reliable awareness measurement in the projection of attitude and purchase intent goals.

In setting attitude and awareness goals and projecting purchase intent, review the level of change in the target market behaviour from the previous years and compare it to the marketing objectives of the plan you are preparing. For example, in previous years you have been averaging 3 percent trial of new purchasers, and your plan now requires that you generate 10 percent trial. The more aggressive the marketing objectives in terms of a change in behaviour, the greater the increase in awareness and attitude goals and purchase intent.

It is very difficult to recommend what the awareness, attitude, and purchase goals should be for a new product or a product for which you have no quantitative awareness and attitude data. However, some basic awareness principles to keep in mind are:

- Target market unaided awareness exceeds target market purchase.
- The higher the percent of the target market required to purchase, the higher the awareness required.
- The greater the number of major competitors in a category, the greater the difference between the percent of a target market that has unaided awareness and the percent that purchase.
- Purchaser unaided awareness is dramatically higher than the non-purchaser unaided awareness-it can vary from two to five times or more.
- The greater the one-product dominance of a target market and the fewer major competitors, the closer the percentage of purchasers to the percentage with unaided awareness of the product.

Relationship of actual purchase to intent, attitude, and awareness:

General principles are very difficult to provide when describing the relationship between awareness, attitude, purchase intent, and actual purchase. However, a starting point—and only a starting point—for defining the total target market goals (purchaser and nonpurchaser) for percent to purchase, purchase intent, attitude, and unaided awareness is the "50% Happening" premise. As shown in the following example, this very subjective premise suggests you begin with the percent of the total target market that you project to purchase and add 50 percent of each level to the next level of the sequence.

There are more exceptions than rules to this "50% Happening" premise, but it is a beginning sequence to follow if you have no data. Keep in mind that if there is a large number purchasing, if the product is very established, and if there is a great deal of positive trending in the marketplace, you will need to add less than 50 percent for each increment. Likewise, you will need to add more than 50 percent under the opposite circumstances. Remember, the "50% Happening" approach is for the total target market. On the other hand, there can be closer to 100 percent difference between the percent purchasing and those that say they "definitely will purchase" for noncustomers and the total target market. Remember, this "50% Happening" is only a starting point, and you will modify the percentage levels at each increment based on your review of Task l. Also, keep in mind that applying a percent to a percent is not mathematically correct and is directional only.

Task 4

Set awareness and attitude Value goals for each tactical tool:

Now that you have set your attitude and awareness marketing communication goals, the final task is to set specific awareness and attitude goals for target customers and noncustomers for each tactical tool. The value goals you assign each tool are very important, because each tactical segment of the marketing plan will be developed to fulfill its respective value goals. The values assigned to each tool will be dependent on what you are marketing and where your product is in the product life cycle. Most important, you will set value goals for each tool based on your specific product situation and its competitive sets in the marketplace. Accordingly, you want to review Task 1 again before you begin setting tactical tool value goals in Task 4.

Rank tactical tools by importance:

Having reviewed Task 1 again and knowing that the value goals you set are very subjective and only a starting point, attempt to rank the tactical tools based on their importance in fulfilling the marketing communication goals. In order to do this: (1) review your tactical experience; and (2) review each tactical tool against the overall marketing strategies and against the respective strategy for each tool, such as personal selling/ service, promotion, and advertising. This will help you determine the degree of emphasis to place on each tool. For example, if the personal selling strategy states "maintain sales force effectiveness comparable to that of the previous year," and the promotion strategy states "increase promotion activity to stimulate trial from new purchasers;" the promotion tool would be given greater importance than in the past relative to the personal selling strategy. The key point to remember is that {(your strategic direction does not call for a change in marketing approach for a particular tool, that tool should not be given more or less importance in this year's plan versus the previous marketing plan.

Having compared one tool to the other, list "important" (I), "moderately important" (MI), or "very important" (VI) next to each tool to indicate its awareness and attitude value. Usually, every tool has some importance, but if you believe a particular tool has no importance relative to awareness and attitude, do not give it an importance ranking. For example, you might decide that, while the "price" tool is "very important" in affecting attitude, it really has no importance in building the overall awareness for the product.

Assign values by importance:

Based on the importance rankings, assign awareness and attitude percentage point values to each tool for purchaser and non-purchaser so that they total to the awareness and attitude marketing communication goals. If you have thoroughly gone through Tasks 1, 2, and 3, as well as the importance ranking process in your assignment of values, you will find some of your tactical tool goals virtually the same, while others will have major disparities. These results are dependent upon what contributions you expect each tool to make in fulfilling the marketing communication goals.

Another point to remember is that if a tactical tool or a group of tactical tools has been given a relatively low goal value, put a minimum of marketing resources against it when preparing this segment of the tactical implementation plan. Unless you can get this tool above the threshold level to make it effective, don't use it. For example, if the advertising communication tools received very low value goals, it might be best to concentrate your resources in personal selling and merchandising (the non-media tools), which are concentrated closer to the purchaser and do not have the higher associated costs. Put your major investment or increased investment against the few tools that will drive your plan.

Expect to revise these value goals as you prepare and interface the tactical tool segments of the plan. For example, you might assign more weight to the advertising media tool after determining that effectively communicating a specific promotion will require not only the merchandising tool via store displays, but also more media via newspaper ads. Further, as you finalise the marketing budget and reconcile it with the sales objectives and bottom-line goals, there most likely will be an adjustment in tactical tool values.

A major question we originally raised and have not addressed is: What is the multiple progression effect of integrated communication among all the tools that truly reinforces the market positioning and drives behaviour?

The best answer is that, because this multiplier effect is virtually impossible to measure, it serves as your communication bonus for the plan, providing the safety margins to compensate for any shortfalls in those tactical tools that do not deliver the expected awareness and attitude communication. Think of it as your "goals" insurance policy in your overall plan delivery of the marketing communications.

Finally, even if you have no data (which is unlikely) or minimal data from which to develop your overall marketing communication goals and tactical value communication goals, it will be a good learning exercise for you and others in your company to arrive at estimates of awareness, attitude, and intent to purchase to fulfil your marketing objectives. Going through this process, even without numbers, will point out the challenges you will face as you proceed to Step 7, the development of your tactical tools. Working through this process will also point out the importance of beginning now to develop a database to help you make many of the forthcoming decisions.

COMMUNICATION CONTROL CHALLENGES AND INHERENT PROBLEMS

Now that you have been exposed to the communication goal method, some communication control challenges and inherent problems that make this method only a start to the process of arriving at overall marketing communication goals and allocating awareness and attitude requirements for the specific tactical tools.

Controlled to Somewhat Controlled to Uncontrolled Communication

There is much you can control in the communication of your product and/or service, such as your advertising message, publicity releases, brand name development, packaging, type of promotion and events, company direct service to customers, and point-of-purchase message. However, there is much communication that you cannot control. The sheer noise level in your particular marketplace can exceed your control. This noise level includes the communication of your message and that of your competition, as well as all of the messages your target market is receiving, both within a particular category and on a geographic basis, in their everyday lives. For example, it is estimated that the average adult is exposed to 200 to 300 ad messages every day.

There are also many other forms of communication that you cannot, or believe you can not, control, such as your competitors' sales forces, promotion, and advertising; the retailer's/ distributor's service level; and independent, third-party communications. For example, a magazine reporter might use your product incorrectly because he did not read the instructions, have a bad usage experience, and then write a negative feature on your product.

Many times you have partial control over what may appear to be uncontrollable communication. In the case of a magazine reporter, perhaps the "facts" sheet sent along with the product and instructions was not enough to properly "prep" the reporter. But a phone call highlighting the instructions could have preceded and followed the sending of the material. Further, some believe that the manufacturer has no control over the retailer's displays. However, having a company representative call the retail contact with examples of how to build a retail display, with corresponding manufacturer's incentive, may provide some control over the retailer's communication of the manufacturer's product. The point is that a well-designed and well-executed marketing plan with detailed follow through can provide some control over what might originally be considered uncontrollable communication and give your product a better chance to succeed.

Addressing the communication control challenges is critical to determining what overall marketing communication is required to move the target person to action and what is required by each tactical tool to deliver the overall communication for the plan. Yes, there is only so much communication you can control, and yes, because of the control challenge, your communication goals and values are only directional. However, the key is to be aware of what you truly cannot control and to make every effort to control as much as you can.

Shortcomings in the Application of Communication Goals

In addition to the communication control challenges one faces when relating behaviour to communication, you should also be aware of the many shortcomings in the application of the communication goals approach.

1. Not all products are alike. Every product, category, and industry is unique, and what applies to one does not-apply to all.
2. Communication is a fluid process. The effect of communication on building awareness, attitude, and usage is very fluid, with much overlap and no real beginning or end. Also, you should remember that the communication and behaviour relationship can be very time sensitive. The time period needed for the process to take effect could be seconds, such as an impulse purchase, or years, such' as purchasing a new auto or home.
3. Subjectiveness is involved in the method application. While we try to quantify throughout the application of this method, you will still need to apply intuitive judgement. Accordingly, another major problem regarding this method arises from

the subjectiveness involved in arriving at the overall marketing communication goals and individual awareness and attitude value goals for each tool.

4. Marketing activities have a cumulative effect. Also, there is the problem of attempting to determine what the overall effect will be on target market awareness and attitude when you combine the communication power of the different tools. Is the whole greater than the sum of the parts? For example, let's say we give the advertising media tactical tool a value goal of achieving 10 percent awareness among the target market, in conjunction with a 10 percent awareness goal for merchandising and a 5 percent awareness goal for publicity. When you combine advertising media with merchandising and publicity, the awareness contributions of each tool combined together are not just additive but many times multiple in effect.
5. Communication effects are difficult to measure. Another problem in the attempt to plan the effects of communication and behaviour on each other relates to measurement. How much does a store display affect awareness and attitude in-store? How much effect does a personal sales presentation have in the awareness and attitude toward the product? What effect does sampling a product have on attitude? Accordingly, it's difficult to measure the effects of communication and behaviour on each other. When it is possible to measure effectiveness, it is difficult to project these findings when planning in different product and market environments.

6

DEVELOPING EFFECTIVE MARKETING PLAN

A marketing plan is an arranged structure to guide the process of determining the target market for your product or service, detailing the target market's needs and wants, and then fulfilling these needs and wants better than the competition. A disciplined marketing planning as a comprehensive, sequential, interlocking, step-by-step decision and action process.

1. The marketing background includes the information base from which the marketing plan is developed.
2. The marketing plan provides direction for the execution in the market place.
3. The marketing execution is the actual interaction with the target market and is responsible for generating the projected sales and profits.
4. The marketing evaluation measures the level of success of the plan's execution and provides learning that is incorporated in the marketing
5. Background section developed for the next year's marketing plan.

The disciplined approach, although initially more time consuming, dramatically increases the chances of your product's or service's success, because the marketing plan prepared in this manner is just that-totally planned. It is a data based plan that is very encompassing, yet feasible to execute. Why do we say employing this disciplined marketing planning methodology increases your chances of success in marketing your product or service? Because this method of marketing planning is:

1. *Disciplined:* To truly integrate marketing tools, one needs a very set methodology to sort out and interface these many overlapping elements. Integrating can become very implicated and, in some instances, overwhelming. Accordingly, disciplined marketing planning employs a sequential, step-by-step system that asks for consideration of all tools and takes the marketing through a clear incremental building process. The sequential steps put the various planning tasks in a logical order so you do not get ahead of yourself. Further, because so much of marketing is not easy to quantify and evaluate, disciplined marketing planning demands that measurable objectives are incorporated throughout your marketing plan. Starting at the top of the marketing plan, there are objectives for sales, marketing objectives, and communication goals, and objectives for every tactical marketing mix tool, such as promotion, advertising, and publicity. Each objective is very specific and quantifiable. If it is not quantifiable and measurable, it is not an objective. Finally, we end the plan with specific evaluation objectives in order to accurately measure the impact of the marketing programme.
2. *Target market driven:* Everything we do to generate sales revolves around the target market. To emphasize this point, the word marketing has "market" within it. Of all the things necessary to be

successful in selling a product, understanding the target market is most important. From start to finish in writing a marketing plan, the target market is the focus determining its needs and wants and fulfilling those needs and wants better than the competition.

3. *Interlocking, not just integrated:* Disciplined marketing takes the integrated marketing approach to the next level by providing a sequential, step-by-step methodology that numerically locks the various elements of the marketing plan together. Each element and marketing mix tool is quantifiably integrated to meet the up-front sales objectives of the plan. No longer should the supporting plan elements and communication tools be woefully inadequate to meet the sales objectives. This happens, for example, when the target market is too small to support the sales objectives or when the advertising media weight is half the amount necessary to generate the level of awareness to affect the target's attitude.

As the preceding cases demonstrate, the sequence of steps is important, because what comes after in the order of the plan is, in effect, making what comes before possible. For example, generating advertising awareness for the message is made possible by the amount of media weight put into the marketplace to communicate the message. Likewise, certain elements of the plan are placed directly next to each other because they have a direct quantitative tie to each other. For example, sales objectives precede the target market(s) and are directly reliant on the size of the target market(s) and their behaviour as detailed in the subsequent marketing objectives.

This interlocking methodology goes beyond integration by directly tying all elements of the marketing plan to each other to fulfil the sales objectives and interlocking many of the tactical marketing mix tools. The result of this interlocking methodology is the effective and efficient execution of a marketing plan.

4. *Comprehensive:* Disciplined marketing requires a comprehensive approach. This includes not only the major components of marketing background and marketing plan, but also the actual execution in the marketplace, where the successes and failures take place. Finally, a comprehensive plan includes a thorough evaluation of each component. This step provides the starting place for next year's plan, effectively closing the loop on this continuous, interlocking, and comprehensive planning process.

Effective marketing cannot take place until every element of the marketing mix is considered and all appropriate elements are incorporated into the marketing plan. Further, because each tactical tool has communication value, each tool must be considered when preparing an integrated communication programme. For example, price is not usually considered a marketing communication tool, yet the price charged for a product communicates something about the product image to the potential purchaser. It has been shown that a substantially higher competitive price charged for a product usually connotes a greater quality image for that product. Accordingly, it takes a comprehensive planning effort to make sure that the communication value of each tactical tool is taken into account and is correctly presented to the target customer.

You will note that each step of the marketing planning process is comprehensive. Beginning with the business review portion of the marketing background section, you will see all the background information that must be gathered, reviewed, and analysed in order to prepare a marketing plan and execute a communications programme. Likewise, the summation of the marketing plan in the form of a final marketing plan calendar and budget is very detailed, ensuring that all necessary elements have been included, properly funded, and described so that there is proper execution in the marketplace. Finally, the evaluation component is very comprehensive to ensure that there is a clear understanding of the effectiveness of the overall plan and the individual components. This allows you to determine what did and didn't work and also learn how to improve on next year's plan by incorporating and reviewing the evaluation data in the business review for next year's planning process.

STEPS TO DISCIPLINED MARKETING PLANNING

To bring order and efficiency to the difficult task of marketing planning, we have broken down the process into ten steps that we believe need to be addressed when developing a disciplined marketing plan. All too often companies think of marketing as only one or two components, rather than as an interlocking, step-by-step, comprehensive process. Following are the ten steps of disciplined marketing planning that we employ.

Step 1

Business review:

To develop a marketing database there first needs to be an understanding of the scope of your business, followed by a comprehensive analysis of the company, product, and marketplace relevant to the target market and competitive situation. This is accomplished through secondary research (company records, data analysis, and existing industry reports) and very often, primary research, including surveys and focus group information. The business review provides a qualitative and quantitative decision-making base for the subsequent marketing plan and a rationale for all strategic marketing decisions within the plan.

Step 2

Problems and opportunities:

The problems and opportunities step is a summary of the challenges that emerge from the marketing database. In this step the data collected from the business review are distilled into meaningful summary points that form the basis of the marketing plan.

Step 3

Sales objectives:

Sales objectives represent projected levels of goods or services to be sold. Setting sales objectives is critical because it is the first task of the marketing plan development and it sets the tone of the entire marketing plan. Everything that follows in the plan is designed to meet the sales objectives, from defining the size of the specific target market and establishing marketing objectives, to determining the amount of advertising and promotional expenses to be budgeted, to the actual hiring of marketing and sales personnel, to the number and kinds of distribution channels/ stores utilised, and, very important, to the amount of product produced or inventoried.

Step 4

Target markets and marketing objectives:

We put the target market and marketing objective steps together because of their critical link to one another.

— *Target Markets:* Once you have developed sales objectives, you must determine to whom you will be selling your product. Making this determination is really defining a target market—a group of people with a set of common characteristics. Target marketing concentrates marketing efforts toward a portion of the population with similar purchasing needs and buying habits.

— *Marketing Objectives:* Marketing objectives clearly define what behaviour you want from the target markets; they are measurable ends that need to be achieved. In this step you will quantitatively lock the required behaviour in the marketing objectives to a quantified target market that will fulfil the sales objectives.

Step 5

Plan strategies:

The overall plan strategies include the positioning strategy for the image of your product and the marketing strategies needed to fulfil the marketing objectives.

— *Brand positioning:* Once you have defined your target market(s) and have established marketing objectives, you must develop a market positioning for your product. By positioning, we mean creating the desired perception of your product within your target market relative to the competition. The positioning strategy provides overall direction for the specific marketing strategies and a singular focus for the tactical marketing mix tools.

— *Marketing strategies:* A marketing strategy is a statement detailing how an individual marketing objective will be achieved. While marketing objectives are specific, quantifiable, and measurable, marketing strategies are descriptive.

They explain how the measurable objectives will be met. In our planning methodology, we outline eighteen strategic considerations that should be addressed in most marketing plans. The marketing strategies also guide the development of the tactical marketing mix tools (Step 7) and provide direction in setting communication contribution values for each tactical tool.

Step 6

Communication goals:

These goals set the target market awareness and attitudes necessary to deliver positioning and fulfil the marketing objectives, as well as provide direction for what is to be accomplished by each tactical tool in terms of communication value.

Step 7

Tactical marketing mix tools:

This step of disciplined marketing planning develops tactical plans. The tactical plans incorporate marketing executions that, when implemented, will allow you to meet your marketing objectives and execute the overall marketing strategies and communication guidelines established earlier. Each marketing mix tool should have its own objectives, strategies, and where appropriate, executional specifics. The following marketing mix tools are included in the tactical planning process.

— *Product:* The product is the tangible object that is marketed to the target market for consumer goods, retail, and business-to-business companies. For service businesses, the product is a future benefit or future promise.

— *Naming:* The naming of the product, service, or company is called branding. A brand or name is the label that consumers associate with your product. For this reason, a brand or name should help communicate the product's positioning and its inherent drama for the consumer.

— *Packaging:* For manufacturers, packaging holds and protects the product and assists in communicating the product's attributes and image. For retailers and service firms, packaging is the inside and outside environment that houses and dispenses the product/services (stores, offices, etc.), and it helps communicate the company's attributes and image.

— *Pricing:* Price is the monetary value of the product. The monetary value is usually governed by what the target market or buyer will pay for the product and what the seller or company must receive for the product in order to defray costs and generate a profit.

— *Distribution:* We define distribution as the transmission of goods and services from the producer or seller to the user. Distribution must ensure that product is accessible to the target market.

— *Personal selling/service:* Personal selling for retail and service firms, often referred to as operations, involves all functions related to selling and service in the store, office, or other environments, such as door-to-door solicitation, in-home selling, and telemarketing. This includes hiring and managing sales personnel, stocking inventory, preparing the product for sale, presenting and maintaining the facility, and follow-up service to the customers.

For business-to-business and package goods firms, personal selling relates to the manufacturer's selling and servicing of its products to the trade and/ or intermediate markets (various buyers of the product within the distribution channel from original producer to ultimate user).

- *Promotion/Events:* Promotion provides added incentive, encouraging the target market to perform some incremental behaviour. The incremental behaviour results in increased short-term sales and/ or an association with the product (e.g., product usage or an event-oriented experience). In addition, promotion is more short-term in focus.
- *Advertising message:* Communication that informs and persuades through paid media (television, radio, magazine, newspaper, outdoor, internet, and direct' mail) constitutes the advertising message.
- *Advertising:* Media Advertising media are paid carriers of advertising, not at the point of purchase. While the advertising message is what is being communicated, the advertising media are how it is delivered.
- *Internet media:* The Internet is an interactive medium with centralised con tent that is delivered to members of the target market when it is requested.

  Members of the target market drive their exposures to your organisation's Internet content, while your organisation drives exposure to its multimedia content.
- *Merchandising:* Merchandising is non-media communication of the company and/or product to the target market. This is the method used to communicate product and promotional information. Merchandising makes a visual and/or written statement about your company through an environment other than paid media, with or without one-on-one personal communication. Merchandising includes brochures, sell sheets,

product displays, video presentations, banners, trade show exhibits, shelf talkers, table tents, or any other non-media tools that can be used to communicate product attributes, pricing, or promotion information.

- *Public Relations:* Public relations creates goodwill for an organisation, not just for the short-term but also regarding long-term public opinion issues. Publicity is a part of public relations and is any non paid media communication that helps build target market awareness and positively affects attitudes for your product or firm. Publicity provides your firm or product with a benefit not found in any other marketing mix tool. Since publicity utilises non-commercial communication, it adds a dimension of legitimacy that can't be found in advertising.

Step 8

Budget, payback analysis, and calendar:

- *Budget*: The budget is the cumulative monetary cost of implementing the plan.
- *Payback:* Analysis An analysis of whether the marketing plan and its specific marketing programmes, as well as executions within the plan, will generate the projected revenues in excess of expenses constitutes the payback analysis.
- *Calendar:* The calendar is a schedule of the marketing plan's tactical executions.

Step 9

Execution:

The tactical execution both for and in the marketplace is developed once the marketing plan is prepared. This is where it all happens-getting your product, service, or store ready for the market and executing the marketing mix tools, such as seasonal selling, the promotion, advertising, merchandising, and publicity. Finally, executorial includes staying on top of all the execution detail in the marketplace. All that you have done will now face the ultimate test of marketplace acceptance. Will the target market buy your product?

Step 10

Evaluation:

The methodology used to help determine the level of success of the overall marketing plan and its specific elements is part of evaluation. We have also included the research and testing components in this step. Research is included because it is a means to evaluation, and testing is a component of this step because it is a learning experience. For example, you might evaluate the effectiveness of a single plan element, such as advertising, or the entire plan in test markets on a limited scale before full implementation.

While evaluation is the last step in the process, it signals a new beginning to the whole disciplined approach, as evaluation findings become a major part of the marketing background section in the preparation of next year's marketing plan. Evaluation is one of the most important steps, because it is a learning tool that will lead to improved marketing plans and execution of marketing programmes in the future.

7

HOW TO PREPARE A BUSINESS REVIEW

A business review will help you compare trends within your company to those of your industry category and key competitors. The industry category is the overall business in which you compete. Throughout the business review, we use the terms consumers and customers. In order to analyse company trends, we need to investigate the behaviour of company customers, those people who have purchased a company's product. If we are to compare company trends to industry category and key competitor trends, we also need to look at the purchase behaviour of consumers, people who have purchased the industry category product, a subset of which is company customers. For business-to-business companies, think of customers as business customers and consumers as business consumers.

IMPORTANCE OF MARKET INFORMATION

Today, consumers have more product choices than ever before. They also have more information about the choices. The combination of more competition and a bombardment of communication from the many competitive alternatives means marketers have to work much harder to affect target market behaviour in today's environment. Thus, it is more important now than at any time in the history of marketing to really understand your target market and to let this understanding drive not only your marketing decisions, but the entire decision-making framework of the company.

Many of the business successes of the past twenty years have come about not because of great business management, but because of individuals with tremendous consumer insight—insight developed through a deep understanding of the target market, the business environment, and the competition. It was the genius of people like Steve Jobs, who understood the impact of the personal computer first on business people and then on home consumers. Jobs started Apple Computer from his garage, igniting the computer revolution.

Much of the target market innovation in today's marketing environment is coming from retailers, service firms, package goods companies, and business-to business firms that are interacting with their target markets with a new level of urgency. Technological innovations in the retail industry, such as "smart cash registers," increased use of research, and marketing databases have provided marketers a wealth of customer information. The more successful business-to-business firms are spending less time selling what they have and more time defining their customers' needs. And package goods companies faced with parity of product and a sales promotion environment are exploring new ways to build brand equity and value-added with their products. Marketers who are on the front lines, engaging in dialogue with the consumer on a daily basis, are the ones who are often closest to the consumer and target market demands. This "closeness" is bringing about a change in the way many marketing-oriented companies are doing business.

These marketing-oriented companies are now in a position to define specific segments based upon unique needs or consumption behaviour and then realistically set marketing objectives to affect the segment's behaviour. For example, companies now have the ability to know whether product repurchase rates are different for new versus old customers or by demographic age segment. They have the ability to determine exactly how many customers there are for each unique purchasing segment, and they know what the, average expenditure per purchase and the average number of purchases is for the segments. With this type of target market information, the marketing-oriented company is able to set objectives to affect consumer behaviour. As a result, the marketers writing the plan know they have a good chance of achieving the goals, because these objectives have been set with the consumer's needs in mind. For example, setting an objective that increases the repeat purchase rate might be developed due to a knowledge that the consumer has the desire and the ability to purchase more if the company made some basic changes in the way it does business. This might require changing the product to satisfy shortcomings in important attributes in order to stimulate increased repurchase. It might mean changing the packaging to allow for easier storage, or it might mean adjusting price to encourage multiple purchases. And, it might mean improving customer service to increase after-sale purchases and repurchases. While all these involve strategic decisions, it is consumer insights that provide the marketer the confidence to set obtainable marketing objectives and to determine the appropriate strategy for achieving them.

The premise of disciplined marketing planning as outlined in this text is that marketing plans focus on the needs of the target market. The business review is the place where the marketer develops a broad understanding of target market insights. Marketing is a broad discipline in which multiple decisions must be made decisions such as which customers should be targeted, through what specific combination of product features, with what price, through what distribution channels, with what type of service, and via what type of communication. However, these decisions cannot be made without a systematic review of all known facts affecting the customer. The business review provides the facts so that sound decision making can be achieved.

ELEMENTS OF THE BUSINESS REVIEW

A well-developed business review should be utilised as a daily reference source. Your business review should be updated each year to reflect the most recent changes in your industry and company. Therefore, if this is your first business review, don't be overwhelmed. If you don't have time to complete all sections, work on those that most affect your business. Then, next year, update those sections and further complete some of the others for which you didn't previously have time. Completing the business review can be more than a one-person job. Request assistance from other people in your company, to help compile the information.

There, are three sections, to a business review:

1. Scope.
2. Product and market review.
3. Target market effectors.

Scope

Scope helps define your core business, it identifies what business or businesses you are in and subsequently, the product or business area of emphasis will then your information search in the business review. Often included, in strategic business plans, this Chapter will serve as a bridge from your strategic plan to the marketing plan. If you do not have a strategic business plan that has addressed this issue you will need to do so in the scope section of the business review. Without this first section, you won't have parameters to guide your information search, For example, a company like Famous, Footwear might pull information on athletic wear trends and footwear trends. While Famous Footwear only sells shoes many competitors also sell athletic wear. However the decision of whether or, not to' also carry athletic wear should be determined before the marketing department starts its planning process by collecting data. If the scope of the business is not decided in a systematic and disciplined manner the business review can quickly become too broad and very unfocused. Worse yet, the availability and mere collection of data can be a self fulfilling prophecy that impacts later decision-making.

However keep in mind as you prepare the next two sections of this business review if you uncover a business opportunity, that is out of the original scope of the business but has tremendous value, we would recommend you keep it in the business review. It might become part of a new product segment in your marketing plan.

Product and Market Review

Product and market review examines the first layer of consumer and customer behaviour. The aggregate behaviour and demand of consumers and customers is identified through a comparison of the industry category, specific, competitors and your company in the area so product, sales, distribution, pricing, and communications, This sectional so provides a historical perspective on the industry, company, and product development.

It details pertinent consumer behaviour trends that will influence future purchasing habits. Finally this section includes the competitive review comparing your company's and/or product performance to the competition

Target Market Effectors

Target market effectors, shifts the focus from overall aggregate industry and company product tends to exploring the consumer and customer segments. This was a necessary a first steps in terms of insight into the consumer because the product performance is the macro view of the consumer's habit. Now, by defining the business in terms of basic consumer and customer segments needs and wants, the business review will become fertile ground for creative decisions making later in the planning process.

PREPARING THE BUSINESS REVIEW

Task 1: Prepare an Outline

It is important to understand that the business review, as presented in this coursepack is broad and attempts to be all encompassing . You must tailor the business review to your specific needs and situation, in terms of both the information you gather and the format in which you provide it. For example, an auto parts manufacturer might include business-to-business information and consumer information if the product has both an original equipment manufacturer and after-market component. A package goods manufacturer may include both a channel track and consumer market analysis. Further, availability and quality of information may dictate the ultimate form of your business review. The outline gives you a framework for gathering the information. Expect the business review to evolve as you go on.

Always start your business review by developing a written outline. The outline should be as specific as possible, covering each major area of the business review. The outline helps you stay focused and ensures that critical data needed for actionable marketing plans will be obtained in a disciplined and sequential process, each section is a step with topical points discussed and explained so that the reader has a full understanding of how to gather and organise this information for use in the marketing plan. The following is an example of an outline for a business review. The first task that you must undertake in an outline tailored to your business and industry.

Task 2: Develop Questions

List questions that need to be answered for each section of the business review outline. The questions will provide direction in determining what specific information you need to accumulate.

Task 3: Develop Data Charts

Develop data charts with headings to help structure your search for relevant information. When completed, the charts should enable you to answer the major questions pertaining to each section of the business review outline. Organise the headings and columns of the charts first in order to determine what information needs to be found prior to the data search. This forces you to look for data and numbers that will provide meaningful information. Remember, if you look for data before developing your charts, you may tend to construct the charts around what is easy to find, not what should be found.

Task 4: Develop Reference Points for Comparisons

Always develop charts that have reference points for comparison so that the data are actionable. For example, when you analyse sales growth for your company, compare this against the sales growth for the industry. In this manner, the company's sales growth can be judged against a reference point. And, remember, a business review should always provide reference points of comparison within the company (past-year trends), between the company and the industry category, and between the company and its key competitors. Whenever possible, include five-year trend information so that the current year's performance can be judged relative to past years' performance. The following provide some basic reminders that are applicable throughout the business review and pertain to the collection and organisation of the data you gather.

Compare five-year trends:

It is important to review trends whenever analysing data that will direct marketing decisions. This allows the marketer to determine not only increases and decreases from year to year, but also shifts in the marketplace over a period of time. For example, while any given product or target market segment may account for the greatest sales volume in one year, a review of five years' worth of data might show that the leader has had flat sales and that another product or target segment will soon dominate the category if the trends continue. Therefore, it is important to look beyond a static one-year number to get a feeling for the fluid nature of data over a period of time.

Trends within the company:

The marketer must be aware of the trends within the company. For example, what customer segment accounts for the most volume? Is this same company segment growing, flat, or declining in volume over the past five years? Is there another company segment that is growing faster and will be the dominant target market in the future? If you have a large company, it is also very insightful to compare regions of the company to the overall company system. This regional review is helpful when determining different local target markets or marketing objectives versus company system target markets or marketing objectives.

Company to industry comparisons:

It is also important to compare the company to its appropriate industry category. Are the target markets that are responsible for the most company product volume the same target segments responsible for the most industry category volume? Is your company's sales trending comparable to, above, or below the industry category across products with the highest sales volume, transaction volume, and profit potential? What are your company's market share trends (your share of sales or transaction volume relative to the industry) overall and among various target market segments?

Competitive comparisons:

Finally, the marketer must also take into consideration the competitive environment and any changes or trends that will make it harder or easier to capture market share against identified target market segments. For example, there might be an increase in the total number of competitors, or a competitor may have developed a product or manufacturing innovation resulting in a price or product attribute advantage.

Benchmark marketing:

Although the concept of comparing relative points of data started in the retail industry, we apply the principles to all business types—retail, package goods, service, and business-to-business firms. One way benchmarking is successfully utilised today is with businesses that have multiple locations or geographic markets. The concept is to find departments, product lines, stores, or markets with similar characteristics, such as product mix and sales potential and then compare results. In order to accomplish this, many firms designate their markets into A, B, and C markets, with each broad market designation demonstrating similar characteristics. Then sales by store, sales by product, customer counts, sales per transactions, purchase ratios, profits, and expenses can be compared across like markets. With this benchmark across a marketer's system, strong and weak performances can be identified and management can take necessary actions based upon exceptions to the average.

Another way benchmarking is used is by comparing target market segment performance. For the American Automobile Association (AAA) we looked at the performance of customer segments based upon age, length of membership, and product use. For example, renewal was considerably lower among members of five years or less than for members of greater than five years. And users of specific AAA products had greater cross-sell into the range of AAA products than others. Again, establishing averages and then comparing target segments to the averages allowed us to do two things:

1. Identify target segments or products not performing to expectations or company averages, with the objective of increasing past performance.
2. Focus on targets or products that were meeting company averages but that had inherent strengths that would allow them to perform significantly better into the future. We use the concept of benchmark marketing in developing a comparison between relative points of data. Although in the past management used the comparisons as reasons for hiring and firing, we use the comparison data as a way to uncover opportunities and focus on solving problems. Therefore, we refer to comparing

relative points of data not as the deadly parallel, but as benchmark marketing. A single piece of data is really of no use to any marketer. The fact that a company experienced a 10 percent sales growth means very little unless compared to some other benchmark, such as the industry category. If the industry category increased 15 percent, the company actually lost market share. Suddenly, the 10 percent sales growth doesn't look so good.

In summary, establishing comparisons within your company and comparing your company to the industry category provides the following benefits:

1. Allows you to identify products and/or target markets that are performing below or above the company average, thus providing insight to further exploit strengths or solve weaknesses.
2. Allows you to identify shifts in target market and product trends within the industry.
3. Allows you to compare or benchmark your firm to your industry, thus providing insight into how you are actually performing versus your competition.

Task 5: Conduct Data Search

Institute a disciplined data search. Stay focused on what needs to be found by constantly reviewing your outline. This will allow you to feel confident that you have compiled all of the existing data necessary to complete your charts.

Task 6: Write Summary Statements

After the charts have been completed, write brief statements summarising the major findings and answering the questions you developed in Task 2. Include a summary rationale when needed. Keep the summary objective by strictly reporting the findings;

don't provide solutions at this point. The business review is not for developing objectives and strategies; it is for providing facts from which to develop a marketing plan and the supporting rationale. However, as mentioned in the Introduction, you should jot down your thoughts and ideas as you prepare your business review to potentially use later when writing your marketing plan.

ORGANISING THE BUSINESS REVIEW

The sections of the final written business review should follow the same sequence as the steps developed in your outline. Each section should include summary statements followed by completed, detailed data charts. Finally, write the marketing background and plan in the third person, being as objective as possible. Do not interject personal feelings that cannot be documented by fact. Write in a very clear, concise manner so that there can be no misinterpretation of what is presented. And don't assume that everyone who reads the plan will have the same base of information as the writer. Include all available information pertinent to the issues being discussed so that everyone reading the plan will have the same frame of reference.

Conducting Research

In preparing your business review, data can be obtained through both primary and secondary research. If you employ a research firm, a marketing communications firm that conducts research, or an in-house research department, primary research is the most effective way of obtaining data specific to your market, your product, and your competitors. If you do not have access to a professional researcher, however, we recommend that you do not try to do primary research yourself, but rather, rely on secondary research, data compiled by outside sources. However, both secondary and primary research be utilised in preparing a marketing database and business review.

Primary Research:

Original research compiled to meet your specific data requirements is broken down into two categories, quantitative and qualitative.

Quantitative Research:

Data and information are usually obtained through surveys, with results gathered from a representative random sample of given universe. The samples are large enough to make inferences that are statistically significant. One is customer-based research, which provides information about a company's own customers. The other is market-wide research, which is used to provide information about the overall category user/ purchaser base.

Qualitative Research:

Research methods that do not statistically represent the target market universe provide qualitative data. Qualitative research typically includes talking with small groups of consumers in the format of focus groups, mall intercepts, and one-on-one interviews. Consumers are asked to provide insights into their likes and dislikes of a particular product and why and how they purchase or use one type of product versus another. Qualitative research is used to gain insights into the strengths and weaknesses of advertising, brand positioning concepts, and other forms of communication.

Qualitative research also adds depth and richness to quantitative findings. For example, quantitative research may determine that a company has a perceived customer service problem relative to the competition. Qualitative research can be used to help further explain what consumers feel customer service entails in the company's particular industry and what specifically is lacking in the company's customer service as compared to that of other companies Another form of qualitative research has gained much acceptance and use, and that is ethnographics. This form of research involves watching consumers as they relate to the company's product. Whether in public places such as airports or in shopping environments, a great deal of information can be learned through these observation techniques.

Finally, a word of caution. Used by itself, qualitative research can be very misleading. It is not statistically based; a roomful of ten people is often a poor representation of what the marketplace really thinks. Qualitative research is most valuable when used to enrich quantitatively defined observations.

Secondary Research:

Secondary research, which may also be quantitative or qualitative, is not specifically compiled for your company; it is existing information that is available through outside sources. An example of a secondary research source is census information. Just as with primary research, combining this type of secondary research information with your company's data will allow you to develop insights into your customers, your market, and the problems and opportunities facing your company. The only difference is that primary research is conducted to answer specific questions a company might have. To answer these questions with secondary research, you may have to dig a little more and be willing to analyse multiple studies to find your answers. Even then, you may not be able to answer all of your questions, so you will have to rely on judgment. Of course, secondary research is also typically less expensive than primary research. In most cases, a mix of both primary and secondary research is appropriate. A secondary search should be completed first, with primary research conducted to fill the voids of the existing data where possible.

Indexing:

Indexing, used extensively in the business review, is a process that presents a number or group of numbers in relation to an average, or base. It is a method of showing a relationship between two sets of numbers or percentages. Indexing is based upon an average of 100. Anything over 100 means the index represents something greater than the average; anything below 100 is less than the average.

When indexing, a base number is established and all other numbers are compared to it. For example, assume 60 percent of the population owns a home and home ownership is further broken down by age category. Since 60 percent is the average percentage of home ownership, it becomes the base number from Which to measure any subset of the population. In this example, among 18- to 24-years-old, only 20 percent own homes; 20 percent divided by 60 percent equals 33. Thirty-three is substantially below 100; thus, 18- to 24-years-old own homes at one-third the average across all ages.

In another example, 30 percent of a national company is consumers live in Bangalore. With that, you would expect them to consume 30 percent of the product (30 divided by 30 equals an index of 100, or average). But if Bangalore consumers consume 60 percent of the company's product, they are consuming at a rate of 60 percent, divided by the base of 30 percent, for an index of 200. Thus, the Bangalore market would compare at twice the national average, or 100 points above the expected consumption pattern.

Sources of Secondary Information:

The following are commonly used sources of information available to most any marketer. They will help you obtain the necessary data to complete the business review portion of your marketing plan. Though this is by no means an exhaustive list of information sources, it is one that most marketing professionals can use without incurring large costs. Many of the references listed can be found in a public or university library, can be obtained free, or can be purchased at a reasonable cost. The sources are found under easy-to-understand category headings:

— *Product user characteristics/Size of market/demographic information:* Sources here provide age, income, and education levels, among other demographic segmentation statistics, which help to define product usage and size of potential markets.

— *Lifestyle segmentation information:* Sources in this section provide attitude, opinion, interest, and lifestyle information to help define target market segments.

— *Media spending/competitive information:* Sources here provide media planning and buying information along with data on competitive spending.

— *Association and trade show information:* Sources in this section provide trade association listings. Many trade associations provide valuable industry data that is useful for compiling a business review.

— *Media and production costs/availability:* Sources provide information required by advertisers for buying media and print production.

8

SETTING OF SALES OBJECTIVES

Sales objectives are self-defining, in that, they represent projected levels of goods or services to be sold. Everything that follows in the plan is designed to meet the sales objectives-from confirming the size of the target market and establishing realistic marketing objectives, to determining the amount of advertising and promotion, to the actual hiring of marketing and sales personnel, to the number and kinds of distribution channels/stores utilised, and, very important, to the amount of product produced or inventoried.

SALES OBJECTIVES MUST BE CHALLENGING AND ATTAINABLE

Because sales objectives have substantial impact on a business, they must be simultaneously challenging and attainable. If they are not, they could have a disastrous effect on short-term, bottom-line profits as well as on the long-term success of the business. If sales objectives are dramatically increased, the cost of doing business will also rise dramatically to accommodate the projected increase in sales. Accordingly, if your sales objectives are set too high and cannot be attained, your resulting expenses to sales ratio will be very high, causing profits to fall below expectations. If you dramatically underestimate your sales objectives and have inadequate production capacity or inventory, you will not be able to sufficiently fulfil demand, meaning opportunity is lost to the competition. Over the long-term, this may translate to the loss of good distributors, loyal customers, and first-time customers.

In summary, a sales objective should be based upon an accurate estimate of the market opportunity and the capacity of the organisation to realise those opportunities.

SALES OBJECTIVES MUST BE TIME SPECIFIC

You must set time-specific sales objectives in order to provide a start and end date for your marketing programme. It is also important to set both short- and long-term sales objectives. Short-term sales objectives are generally for one year or less, while long-term objectives usually have a time frame of a minimum of three years. Long-term sales objectives are needed to plan the future direction of the company or product in such areas as equipment, real estate, personnel, and capital. Further, what you include in year one of your marketing plan will affect sales objectives set for years two and three. Testing new products and service programmes in year one might be required in order to meet sales objectives in year three.

SALES OBJECTIVES MUST BE MEASURABLE

Setting measurable sales objectives provides the means for determining what must be included in your marketing plan and for evaluating its success. Accordingly, sales objectives are quantified in terms of money and units for manufacturing firms, money and transactions (and occasionally units) for retail firms, and money and persons served for service firms. You must set sales objectives, transactions or persons served. Sales cover your expenses and provide a profit, and they reflect the impact of any increase or decrease in/the price of your product. Units/transactions/ persons served indicate the fundamental health of your business. If you are continually projecting increased sales but decreased unit sales, you will eventually experience a decline in sales, because price increases will no longer compensate for the loss of unit sales.

Projected profits, a direct result of sales, should also be included along with sales objectives. Accordingly, as the author of this plan, you must have an understanding of profit expectations in order, to effectively prepare and evaluate the marketing plan.

For a non-profit organisation, the goal might be the funds raised to support its programmes. In a government agency such as an employment service, it may be number of job placements. Or for a political campaign manager, it may be per cent of votes cast for your candidate by county or district. Whatever the organisation, there must be sales objectives or a simulation thereof.

QUANTITATIVE AND QUALITATIVE FACTORS AFFECTING THE SETTING OF SALES OBJECTIVES

Both quantitative and qualitative factors must be taken into consideration in the development of sales objectives. Quantitative factors, inputted first, are hard numbers based upon objective, historical data. Qualitative factors are more subjective due to non availability and difficulty in quantifying certain types of information. Therefore, interpretation of these additional subjective factors leads to an adjustment of the quantitatively based sales objectives.

Quantitative Factors Sales Trends

When you're preparing to set sales objectives, the past is

a good place to start. The trending of the market and company sales will be major factors to consider when projecting sales. Market Sales Review the trending of the market over the past five years in terms of money and unit sales. Has the trending of the marketplace been upward, downward, flat, or erratic? Within the total market history of sales and units, what has the trending been of market segments that make up the total market? If you were tracking total market shoe sales, you might have found a flat to slowly upward-trending market, but athletic sales as a subset trending upward at a percentage rate more than twice that of the total market. Accordingly, if you were selling athletic shoes in your store, you would take this trend into consideration when setting objectives.

— *Company Verses Market Sales:* Next, compare how your company's sales are trending year to year versus the total market's sales. In most instances, project your sales to equal or surpass the market rate of growth; otherwise you will be losing share of market.

— *Market Share Trends:* Another factor to consider is the trending of your market share for the company/ division, for the product line and each product, or for the retail/ service category and each major department. At what rate has your share of total sales been trending relative to the market? Has it been growing in a growing market? Has your share been going up in a market that is shrinking? Or has your share of market been decreasing in a declining market? If you find that your product is losing snare in a market that is declining, it would be unrealistic to project sales increases unless your strategy is to reverse this trend through a major marketing commitment. When setting sales objectives keep in mind that not only is it difficult to reverse a product's sales decline in a one-year period, but it is also extremely difficult to reverse a product's decline within a declining market.

Size and Purchase Rates of Target Market

A good double-check of the methods just cited in the determination of accurate sales objective estimates is an independent appraisal of the size and purchase rates of the target market for your product or service. Many new business ventures and good new products fail because of an overly optimistic estimate of the size and trending of the market. It is very important to review census and industry data, as well as primary research if available, in your business review to determine how big the market really is and how it is trending.

Sales objectives often are set too high year after year because the company's management does not recognise a continual erosion of the target market, an erosion that could have been documented through published industry data, company sales data, and/or primary research. Through primary research, our agency was able to document for a fabric chain that the number of women who sew garments declined approximately 5 per cent per year over a ten-year period.

Many times, particularly with new products and the development of entire new market categories, there is limited market data and no company sales data on which to project sales objectives. In these instances, you use a simulation approach and track sales growth of categories and/or companies in different, but somewhat related, product and market situations.

Budget, Profit, and Pricing Considerations

In determining realistic sales objectives, it is helpful to have an understanding of your company's historical operating budgets and profit expectations. Ideally, sales cover expenses and provide for profits. The simple fact is that you need a minimum level of sales to stay in business and grow. For this reason, the cost of doing business, or expenses incurred to operate your business, is an important quantitative factor to consider when setting your sales objectives. Along with that input, planned product price increases or decreases must be factored into all sales objectives, because they dramatically affect sales volume and profitability.

Qualitative Factors

Economic considerations:

One factor affecting sales objectives that is difficult to forecast is the economy. Adjust your sales objectives based on your estimation of the economic factors that will directly affect your business. Are you forecasting sales for a recessionary, inflationary, or relatively stable period? If you are projecting sales for an inflationary period, you will probably be estimating sales to increase at a greater percentage than unit sales. Interest rates are also an important factor in establishing sales objectives. Businesses that rely heavily on their customers' purchasing on credit, such as auto dealers and real estate firms, usually see their sales slump as interest rates rise. In addition, you must plan accordingly for any major changes in the tax laws. For example, elimination of an investment tax credit for heavy machinery would affect the sales of companies manufacturing heavy equipment.

Competition:

What you identified as a large and growing market can be diluted by strong and growing competition. Before finalising sales objectives, review the competitive data in the Product and Market Review section of your business review. Has a major competitor noticeably expanded its sales force, increased the number of trade deals to retailers, added distribution channels/ store locations, changed its product mix, or introduced a new product or service? Based on your competitive review of advertising media, is the competition increasing or decreasing its level of spending? Increased competitive advertising spending, particularly in a consumer marketplace dominated by a few major competitors, can negatively affect the chance of your marketing programme's meeting its sales objectives. It is often difficult to determine the direct impact on sales of an increase in competitive advertising. At this point, telephone survey research of your potential market can quantify its impact on your sales. Through this type of research, we were able to measure a 50 per cent increase in awareness for our client's direct competitor. We then translated this awareness into increased sales for the competition and an erosion of our client's market share. Accordingly, an anti competitor plan, along with a revision of the short-term sales objectives, was recommended for our client.

Fad Volume

While it is difficult to forecast, many businesses must deal with "fad" or erratic sales volume. You must learn to recognise and deal with it realistically when setting your sales and profit objectives. Fad volume could be occasional, such as a convention or sports tournament that brings an incremental number of people to your town and your restaurant. Fad volume could also be much longer lasting, such as that created by a highly publicised health care study indicating that the use of fish oil and/ or aspirin prolongs life. Likewise, when there is an event that has negative effects on your short- and/or long-term sales, you must factor in its effects when projecting sales. If your company markets products that are affected by positive or negative fad volume movement, you must estimate the impact of this phenomenon in terms of volume over time. How many consumers will it affect and for how long?

Product's Life Cycle

Another consideration when setting sales objectives is to review where your product is in its life cycle. Do you have a new product with a large untapped target market, minimal competition, and substantial growth potential? If the product was successfully introduced, are the product's sales still growing, have they plateaued, or are they in decline? Your short-term sales objectives should reflect the current life-cycle stage of your product, while your long-term objectives should concurrently reflect the stage of the life cycle into which your product is moving. Many times, to assure a clearer picture of where your product is in its life cycle, it is wise to stand back and review competitive products or draw comparisons to different products with similar characteristics in other industries. After these companies introduced their products, at what rate did they grow, when did they level off, and at what point in their existence did they decline? By determining if specific products they sell are in a growth, plateau, or declining stage, manufacturers and service firms, as well as retailers, can more accurately forecast expected sales growth for their companies.

Mission and Personality of Your Organisation

An important qualitative factor to consider is the mission and personality of your organisation. What are your company's expectations? What is its reason for being? What is its philosophy of doing business? Is your company conservative and careful or a moderate risk taker? Is it an old-line, "don't rock the boat" company, or a young and charging, "we can do it". Also consider the aggressiveness of your organisation in terms of growth and innovation-product improvements, new products, and the opening of new distribution channels and new markets. Take all of this into consideration when estimating future sales.

Marketing Plan Expectation

Somewhat related to organisation personality is another very important qualitative factor—your initial expectation of the overall marketing effort dictated by your marketing plan. The employment of a new, well-integrated, disciplined marketing plan will usually generate incremental sales, everything else being equal. Further, you would adjust your sales objectives upward if you intend to change the way you market your product, such as improving your product, adding promotional costs, or lowering the price of the product.

METHODOLOGY OF SETTING SALES OBJECTIVES

The methodology of setting sales objectives is both quantitative and qualitative, which means your sales objectives will be a composite of data-based estimates and educated guesses. If you use a disciplined process in setting sales objectives, these goals will be based more on realistic estimates and less on guessing.

Process of Setting Sales Objectives

The recommended process to set your sales objective(s) is based on three tasks:

1. Set individual sales objectives using three different quantitative methods.
2. Reconcile these different quantitative goals into composite sales objectives.

3. Adjust the quantitatively based composite sales objectives through the inter-polation of the relevant subjective qualitative factors, such as the economy, competition, and the personality of your organisation.

Task 1: Set Quantitative Sales Objectives:

We suggest that, if the data are available, you use the following three different quantitative methods: outside macro, inside micro, and expense plus. Each method will help you develop a sales objective estimate, and each estimate will provide one of three parameters from which to make realistic judgments in arriving at your final sales objective(s). Each method can be used exclusively in arriving at a sales objective; however, the final outcome will not be as reliable as when you apply all three approaches. By using the three different approaches, you develop sales objectives derived from three different sets of data-a safeguard against using only one set of data that might not be totally reliable or complete.

Outside macro approach:

In this approach, first look outside your immediate company environment and estimate total market or category sales for each of the next three years. Then, estimate your company's current and future share of the market for the next three years. Finally, multiply the total market or category projections by the market share estimate for each of the next three years to arrive at your sales objectives. You should end up with a three-year projection for both unit and sales.

In order to arrive at these estimates, begin with a review of the data from the past five years for each marketplace in which your product, service, or retail store competes. (If five years of sales data are not available, use what data you have and supplement with available data from similar businesses to arrive at a trending of the marketplace.) If the market is trending up at a 5 per cent rate, you could project the market to continue to grow at this rate for each of the next three years.

Market trend line sales projection:

Rather than applying a straight percentage increase to arrive at market volume for future years, you can statistically project a market trend line. For example, if you were projecting sales in for 2008 and you had a market change from Rs. 4 crore in 2000 to 4.5 crore in 2007, you would perform the following calculation:

Market change 2000 to 2004 = Rs. 50 lakh (4 crore to 4.5 crore)

Market change period = 4 years (2000 to 2004)

Average Rs change per year = 12.5 lakh (Rs. 50 lakh + 4)

Rs change for 8-year period (2000 to 2008) = Rs. 1 crore (12.5 lakh x 8)

Projected Rs sales for 2008 = Rs. 5 crore (4 crore from base year 2000 + Rs 1 crore for change over 8-years period)

This method of projecting sales, referred to as freehand, is the simplest method of determining trend lines. If there is a substantial fluctuation in past sales year by year, you can arrive at a mathematically generated trend line by using the least squares method. For guidance in applying the least squares method, we suggest you refer to a text on business statistics.

Company/product trend line share projection:

To arrive at a share-of-market estimate, review the change in your company's share over the past five years and project a similar share change for the future. You can estimate a percentage point change or use the same freehand approach shown in the preceding example.

Inside micro approach:

Having reviewed the outside market sales, next review your own organisation's sales history. Start at the top, or with a review of your organisation's total sales. Using the straight percentage increase or the trend line approach, arrive at projected three-year sales for your company. From the top go further, and using the straight percentage or trend line approach, estimate sales for each product or department, adding the projected sales of each product/ department together for a three-year company total. Reconcile this total with your initial sales estimate for the entire organisation to determine an ultimate top projection.

Based on history and changes in the marketplace, estimate sales for each bottom-up sales generator and add them together to determine each year's projection. You can use the straight per cent change or trend line approach for each year's projection. However, if you have either too much or very little data to process, you might have to estimate, rather than calculate, each sales projection.

If you are in a manufacturing business, your bottom-up generator becomes the distribution channel (direct accounts, wholesaler/distributors, etc.). If you are in the retail business, build up to a total sales estimate by estimating by store, by market, and by district/region. Use this same approach if you are in the service business. It is often a good idea to have participation from the sales force or the retail service people in the field, as they estimate sales in their area of responsibility.

To arrive at a final micro sales objective, you must then reconcile the organisation's sales estimates derived from the top with those derived from the bottom.

Expense plus approach:

Once you have the outside, macro-based estimates and the inside, microbased sales estimate, it makes good sense to estimate the sales level needed to cover planned expenses and make a profit. This budget-based sales objective approach is more short term in nature and is most useful in helping to arrive at your one-year sales objective. However, you can develop sales objectives for each year of a three-year sales period by employing this approach. A sales objective derived from expense and profit expectations can differ substantially from a sales objective generated from a market or company sales trend projection. This difference in projections may signal the need for a more conservative or aggressive marketing plan. Although very simplistic, it is also very real, because it details the sales that have to be generated in order to stay in business and make a profit.

To arrive at a sales objective using this method, you will need budget data. If your company has been doing business for a number of years, it is relatively easy to estimate expenses and expected profits for the next year by reviewing your historical financial data. It is a good learning experience, particularly if you are new in the business, to review the cost of goods, operating margins, expenses, and profits within the industry and for other comparable businesses. Industry guidelines such as these are available from libraries, trade associations, and the Business Census.

A number of methods can be used to develop a budget-based sales objective. With "expense plus," a common approach that we apply in our business, you first estimate your operating expenses (marketing, administrative, etc.) for the upcoming year. Next, subtract your expected profit (pretax) percentage from your expected gross margin percentage (Gross Sales–Cost of Goods Sold = Net Sales; Net Sales + Gross Sales = Gross Margin) to determine an estimated expense percentage. The gross margin percentage is available from historical company records and/or from industry guideline data. The estimated expense percent is divided into the estimated expense to determine the required sales necessary to meet expense and profit goals.

9

IDENTIFY TARGET MARKET SEGMENTS

Once you have developed sales objectives, you must determine to whom you will be selling your product. Making this determination is really defining a target market—a group of people or companies with a set of common characteristics. Target marketing allows for a concentration of effort against a portion of the universe with similar descriptors, product needs, or buying habits.

Companies don't sell products; customers purchase them. In effect, your company exists because of the customers or target markets you choose to serve. Since we define marketing as the process of identifying the target market(s), determining the needs and wants of the target market(s), and fulfilling those needs and wants better than the competition, the determination of the target market is the most critical step in the marketing planning process.

Your business review analysed potential target markets by looking at many industry category and company target segments responsible for product sales volume. The biggest marketing mistake is to attempt to be all things to all people. It is in this section that the marketer must decide which target segment(s) will form the core of the business and receive the emphasis of effort and budget. The targets are the key to all that follows in the marketing plan, because your target markets are the reason for your product's existence and the key to finding marketing answers. Let your target market drive your marketing plan.

SEGMENTATION

Segmentation is a selection process that divides the broad consuming market into manageable customer or non-customer groups with common characteristics. Segmentation provides the marketer the opportunity to exploit these common characteristics of the consumer or customer group through the company's marketing efforts. Instead of marketing to the "average" consumer, you are able to pinpoint specific clusters of consumers who have unique, yet similar, demographics, lifestyles, attitudes, concerns, purchasing habits, or needs and wants. The most effective marketing communication is essentially the one-on-one sales call, where the skilled salesperson can address the needs of the individual prospect. Due to the similarities inherent in a given segment, marketers too can address groups as if they were communicating with individuals, and direct communications to groups of consumers with similar characteristics via more meaningful products, pricing, and messages. Thus, segmentation allows you to realise the greatest potential sales at the lowest cost.

There are two broad segments for most businesses within which you will develop additional sub-segments for targeting:

1. *Current customers*: Customers and segments of the customer base with whom you' are currently doing business.
2. *New customers*: Segments in which you are not currently doing business or in which you feel there is potential to do more business.

Before you start developing additional target market segments within the two broad segments listed here, think about what you are trying to achieve. More than simply looking for consumer or customer similarities, segment identification involves identifying similarities that are directly tied to sales and profits. When you develop target market segments, you do so by grouping like segments of customers or potential customers, with the objective of finding those segments that are responsible for the most profit, or purchases and that also demonstrate future potential. If you completed your business review, this work has been done. You now just need the parameters that help you make the right target selections.

SHORT-TERM AND LONG-TERM TARGET MARKET SEGMENTS

Remember to develop short-term segments (those responsible for sales within the next year) and also distinct, long-term segments (those that you wish to develop over the next two to three years but that will not account for significant sales in the short term). Long-term target markets typically require significant changes in product, distribution, or operational requirements prior to your effectively satisfying the customers in these groups.

Primary and Secondary Target Markets

When you develop your target market segments, remember that there are varying degrees of importance among the target segments. We group these segments into primary and secondary target markets. While the spending and focus emphasis is different for primary and secondary targets, both are responsible for generating sales. Primary targets typically have greater spending emphasis and contribute to generating sales at far greater rates than secondary target markets.

Primary target market:

A primary target market is your main consuming group. These consumers are the most important purchasers and users of your product and will be the mainstay of your business. In some cases, the primary target market is the heavy user (one-third or less of the purchasers who account for two-thirds or more of the purchases). For companies that are more niche oriented, the primary target will be a smaller, though viable, section of the market that requires selective or specialised goods and services. And in some situations, there will be a primary target market that is an intermediate channel, such as a distributor, and a primary target that is a consumer or end user. Both targets will have different ties to sales and both will require separate plans.

The following criteria should be fulfilled before you finalise a primary target market choice:

– Make sure the customer base is large enough in terms of actual numbers of consumers and volume of purchases. What percent of the product category's volume does your primary target market consume? Given your projected market share, is it enough to support your business? A common reason for a plan's failure is a target market that is too small and limiting. Ideally, try to get your primary target market profile to be accountable for approximately 30-50 percent of the category volume. For example, if 18- to 24-years-old accounted for only 10 percent of the consumption, the marketer would need to expand the age criteria beyond 18- to 24-years-old until the age group was broad enough to account for more volume. However, if the purchase behaviour or the purchasing criteria were distinctly different among 18-to 24-years-old than among other age groups, the marketer would need to establish a number of smaller target markets something that is much more difficult and expensive to execute.

The 30-50 percent criterion can be lower if you are going to specialise against a more narrow purchaser/user base but obtain a larger market share against this segment. However, you must be certain that your company has some special tie to the narrow niche that will command loyalty.

- Make sure the target market is profitable. Determine that the target market purchases sufficient quantity to assure profitability.
- Try to estimate the trending of your primary target market. Is it a growing or shrinking segment? If it is shrinking, will the market be large enough to support your business at its current market share in five years? If not, this should be a danger signal.
- Make sure that your primary target market can be narrowly defined by one unified profile. The primary target market should be a group of individuals or companies with the same basic identifiers and purchasing behaviour. This will allow your marketing effort to be focused against essentially one type of individual.

The primary target market becomes the company's reason for being. You are in business to determine the primary target market's wants and needs and to provide for those wants and needs better than your competition. This pertains to providing the product, service, shopping or sales environment, distribution channel, and price structure that is required by the customer for purchase. The better the definition and description of the consumers in your primary target market, the better you will be able to market to them.

Secondary target markets:

Most plans will identify multiple target markets. The primary target markets receive priority and a majority of the marketing spending, because they will most directly influence the short-term financial success of the plan. The secondary target markets are also important, because they provide additional sales and/ or influence on the sales to the company beyond that of the primary target market as well as future sales to the company. A secondary target market can be one of the following:

- A segment currently too small to be a primary market but shown to have future potential. In some cases, you may identify segments with great growth potential but that currently are very small in absolute purchasing power. In other cases, there might be a large segment that would become a primary target as a result of fundamental marketing changes making your product or service more attractive to this market.
- A demographic category with a low volume but a high concentration index. Often there is a distinct demographic category that accounts for a small percentage of the volume but contains a high concentration of purchasers. For example, 18- to 24-years-old may account for only 10 percent of the total product category purchases, but 50 percent of the 18- to 24-years-old may purchase the product. This may be due to popularity of the product among this age group but fewer total purchase occasions or purchase of more inexpensive product models. In any case, a great percentage of the target uses the product, providing the opportunity for efficient use of marketing and little wasted coverage in targeting the segment.

— Subsets of purchasers or users who make up the primary target markets. As stated in the previous section, your primary target market should ideally be one unified profile of customers accounting for greater than 30 percent of the category volume. This allows for a focusing of resources and message in the marketing effort. However, there are situations in which the volume of any one target market is not substantial enough to qualify it as a primary target market. In addition, each smaller target market has different demographics, needs, wants, product usage, and purchasing behaviour. An example of this is in the target market we developed for a regional menswear retailer.

The retailer was selling primarily suits and sport coats. There were many purchasing profiles, but no single profile group provided enough volume to allow for targeting against that group. The primary target market became very broad and encompassed businessmen who were 18 to 54 years of age. However, the following secondary target markets were developed, with subsequent marketing emphasis and programmes against each.

— Men, 18 to 24, college graduates, entering the working world and looking for affordable suits.

— Men, 45-plus, higher income, at the top of their profession, interested in quality menswear and needing to update their wardrobes.

— Women 18 to 34; women have a great influence over men's purchases of suits and sport coats. Spouses also purchase a substantial number of sport coats as gifts and accompany men in more than 50 percent of their shopping trips, serving as advisors.

- Blue-collar males who need an all-occasion suit; price is a concern.
- Target markets were also broken out by type of profession, as this helped dictate quantity and style of suit purchases.

Influencers:

Influencers can be a primary or secondary target market, though in most situations they are a secondary target market. These are individuals who influence the purchase or usage decision of the primary target market.

A good example of this is the influence children have on their parents in the purchase of many consumer goods, from toys to fast food. Another example is the influence of architects in the use of precast concrete. While the general contractor and the engineer make the actual purchase decision, the architect has tremendous influence both up front in the design of the building and in the final selection of materials.

Influencers are of particular importance in public sector marketing, where outside forces can affect the success of an organisation's marketing programme. In a statewide bus transit marketing effort, we concentrated marketing efforts against current and potential riders as our primary target, but we also targeted opinion leaders, major employers, and education leaders, all of whom affect communities' public support of the bus system, as our secondary market.

In business-to-business situations, a secondary target can often be a customer who currently does not purchase heavily from your company but who has high purchasing potential. You can delineate the potential of this customer by estimating your competitors' sales to this customer and determining what additional needs your company can fulfill for this customer.

Further, manufacturers most often include an intermediate channel as a secondary target segment. This target might be a fabricator, distributor/wholesaler, or retailer that should receive special attention in order to make sure the product is available for the end user to purchase. This is particularly true in marketing consumer goods, with minimal retail shelf space available and multiple competitors selling the same type of product. Often, so much time and money is devoted to selling to the end user that the intermediate channel is taken for granted.

Conversely, many business-to-business manufacturers, because they are selling directly to an intermediate target market (which is their primary target), push these products through the primary distribution channel (often using low prices and promotions) and put less marketing emphasis on the end user to pull the product through the channels. It might be more efficient in the short-term to push the product through intermediate markets. However, the end user should not be totally ignored, as this may mean a loss of demand and loyalty for your product or brand over the long-term.

Purchaser and/or User Determination

Many times the purchaser of a product is different from the user. If this is true in your situation, you need to decide who has the major influence over the actual purchase. Does the one who drinks the beer request a special brand, or does the beer drinker drink what the shopper purchases? In most cases, the individual who does the purchasing becomes the primary target market. However, when the purchaser primarily buys what the user requests, then the user receives primary attention. You must determine whether the primary target group will include purchasers, users, or both. However, keep in mind that it is very difficult (not to mention expensive) to effectively market against two primary markets. Because this is an encompassing step in the defining process, step back and attempt to determine which of these two targets is the driving force and what makes up their purchase and usage behaviour. Consider these two factors in your determination:

1. The inherent benefits of your product to one target or the other.
2. Who the competition chooses as its target market.

TARGET SEGMENTATION METHODOLOGY

The methodology for determining either current customer or new customer segments involves seven tasks. Note that the following methodology is designed for a target that consumes a group of products within the scope of an industry (i.e., shoes for the family or a range of accounting services, etc.). If you have one product, the same methodology applies, except you eliminate Task 1 and Task 6 and start with Task 2, listing the segments for your one product.

Task 1: Sales/profits

The target market process starts with identifying industry and company products that demonstrate strong demand and sales growth. Refer to the business review and list the products that had the most category and/ or company sales, profits, or transactions and are demonstrating the most growth.

Task 2: Segments

We determine target markets by first focusing on the target market segments responsible for purchasing or using the products that meet the following tests:

1. Account for the greatest industry and company product sales volume, and/or profits, and/or transactions, and/or number of customers.
2. Are there industry or company growth products that are trending up in sales, and/or profits, and/ or transactions, and/or customers and that are estimated to be major volume producers in the future.

The segmentation process we use starts by looking at the two broadest segments that account for sales of the products identified in Task 1.

— Current customers.

— New customers (potential customers).

Refer again to the business review to determine the number of current customers and noncustomers that consumed the products identified in Task 1.

List the number of customers and potential customers in the target market, the average price per purchase occasion, the purchase per customer, the number of purchase occasions/number of purchases per year, the penetration (customers as a percent of the potential total category consumers), the retrial rate, and the growth trends in terms of customers/ consumers using or purchasing the product.

Now break the large segments (customers and noncustomers) into smaller segments, looking for characteristics that predict volume. Note the volume of each segment along with the specifics just identified for each of the segments. Finally, list and describe the first two or three segment descriptions that account for the most purchases, profits, transactions, and/or customers.

New customer segments may be identical to current customer segments if you find you still have plenty of customer market share or penetration potential. For example, a customer target market may be 18- to 24-years-old college students, yet your business review shows that you have only 20 percent of a particular state's college students as customers. Obviously, the target market can still be mined for new customers in that state. New trial segments may also be strong industry category segments in which you don't do well but where the segment's purchasing needs or criteria match your product's attributes. Therefore, it makes sense to target poorer-performing customer segments that are relatively strong performing industry segments, especially if the competitive environment is not fiercely intense.

Based upon your findings, you may want to alter your initial target market profile description to more closely mirror the product category's target market in order to expand your current customer base. For example, through an analysis for a retail client experiencing low sales per store, we found that its customer target market was primarily blue-collar with an annual income of under Rs. 15 lakh, while the majority of purchasers in the total category were white-collar with annual incomes over Rs. 20 lakh, skewing to Rs. 30 lakh plus. The analysis involved in this example may also point out the major differences between the customer profiles of your company's product and those of the category and provide insight as to why your company is successfully capturing a specific segment of the product category and how to attract even more of the same consumers.

On the other hand, based upon your analysis, you may want to target a smaller, but growing, segment not targeted by the competition. Factors such as favourable size and growth of the market, above-average expenditures per customer, and the strong awareness and positive attribute ratings of your company might lead you to focus on a segment that does not mirror the category's heavy user target segment.

Task 3. Awareness

Refer to the business review to determine if there is average to above-average awareness for your company and/or products among the segments you are considering for your target market (s).

Task 4. Attitudes

Go back to the business review to determine if the segments in Task 2 have positive attitudes across the most important purchase criteria for each segment. If not, you will need to make a significant effort to change attitudes across the most important purchase attributes in order to convince the segment to purchase in meaningful numbers. Remember, it's always easier to build on strengths than to change a weakness.

Task 5. Decision Criteria

Now, make a decision to target all or some of the segments that provide you the following:

- Strong industry and company sales or growing company or industry sales.
- Positive attitudes toward your company or brand.
- Large size or large potential size (smaller numbers of company customers but large industry category consumers or potential customers).
- Strong money-per-customer average, more profit per customer, or high transactions per customer.
- Loyal segments with strong retrial rates. If the segments in Task 2 do not meet all of the criteria, look for those that have the greatest combination of them.

Task 6. Product Mix of Segments

Look at the mix of products consumed by these segments. Not all of the products in the mix will be the highest-volume, fastest-growing, or most profitable products, but since that's where you started, you will be assured that the final product mix will be of significant volume.

Target Market Versus Product Plans:

This task forces you to develop target market plans and not simply product marketing plans. By looking at the natural mix of products the target market consumes within the scope of your business, you are forced to analyse your company's mix of product offerings to the target market later in the plan. Target market plans lead you to market a mix of product/ service offerings to the consumer, while product plans are much more focused on selling only what you have-one product or service at a time. Ideally, you will pick final segments that perform positively on a majority of the preceding steps. This allows the marketer to essentially minimise the number of weaknesses that must be addressed and to market to segments that have the greatest potential to be profitable and are predisposed to purchase your product.

Task 6 is critical, for it moves you back to developing target market plans rather than product plans. If we looked only at the largest-volume products (Task 1) and defined the target markets from those products (Task 2), we would essentially be developing plans on a product-by-product basis. But in Task 6, we review what group or mix of products these customers of the high volume purchase. Once we detail the mix of products, we are now in a position to write a target market plan that attempts to affect target market behaviour toward the entire mix of products this segment consumes.

Task 7. Demand Analysis

The last step in determining target markets is to attempt to calculate the demand for your product in your chosen target market segments. The demand analysis is a check to make sure that the target segment is large enough to warrant your effort. The conclusions will be directional and are intended to provide you with a rough estimate of the size of your market and the potential business you might generate. It should give you a first check to make sure the sales goals you set in the plan are realistic and obtainable. The following list outlines the procedures to take in estimating demand for your product.

1. *Target market*: How many consumers are in your target market? Define the target market in terms of numbers of potential customers. For example, if your target market is women 25 to 49, provide the total number of women 25 to 49. This is the top-level figure of potential customers. It can be used for calculating future or potential demand.
2. *Geographic territory*: How many consumers are in your defined trading area or geographic market territory? Define your geographic territory and determine the number of your target market customers in this area.
3. *Consumption constraints:* What consumption habits exist that limits the potential customer base of your target market? Determine if there are consumption constraints that will reduce the target market for your product. For example, apartment dwellers have no real need for garden tools or lawn mowers. From this review, develop a final estimate of customers in your geographic territory.
4. *Average purchase per year per customer*: Determine the average number of purchases of your product per year. From the business review and the purchase

rates/buying habits section, you should have access to the average number of purchases per year for your product category.

5. *Total purchases per year in category*: What is the total number of purchases made by the target market in your geographic territory per year? Multiply the number of customers in your territory by the average number of purchases per year to get total purchases.

6. *Average price*: Determine the average price of your product. Utilize the pricing section of the business review to obtain this information.

7. *Your company's share of purchase:* What is your company's market share? Is it trending up or down? Review market share data and trends from the sales analysis, and competitive market shares, strengths, and weaknesses from the competitive analysis section of your business review. Also, consider loyalty measures from the target market effectors/trial and retrial section of the business review.

8. *Additional factors:* What additional factors are there that strongly affect demand for your product? What competitive factors will affect demand? How and why will recent or expected changes in these factors change demand for your product? Additional factors that correlate to the demand for your product, such as a new competitive set, the state of the economy, demographic fluctuations, or changing consumer tastes and lifestyles, should be analysed for their effect on the demand for your company's product.

10

PRODUCT DECISIONS

In marketing, the term "Product" is often used as a catch-all word to identify solutions a marketer provides to its target market. We will follow this approach and permit the term "product" to cover offerings that fall into one of the following categories:

— *Goods:* Something is considered a good if it is a tangible item. That is, it is something that is felt, tasted, heard, smelled or seen. For example, bicycles, cellphones, and donuts are all examples of tangible goods. In some cases there is a fine line between items that affect the senses and whether these are considered tangible or intangible.

— *Services:* Something is considered a service if it is an offering a customer obtains through the work or labour of someone else. Services can result in the creation of tangible goods (e.g., a publisher of business magazines hires a freelance writer to write an article) but the main solution being purchased is the service. Unlike goods, services are not stored, they are only available at the time of use (e.g., hair salon) and the consistency of the benefit offered can vary from one purchaser to another (e.g., not exactly the same hair styling each time).

- *Ideas:* Something falls into the category of an idea if the marketer attempts to convince the customer to alter their behaviour or their perception in some way. Marketing ideas is often a solution put forth by non-profit groups or governments in order to get targeted groups to avoid or change certain behaviour. This is seen with public service announcements directed toward such activity as youth smoking, automobile safety, and illegal drug use.

While in some cases a marketer offers solutions that provide both tangible and intangible attributes, for most organisations their primary offering—the thing that is the main focus of the marketing effort—is concentrated in one area. So while a manufacturer may offer intangible services or a service firm provides certain tangible equipment, these are often used as add-ons that augment the organisation's main product.

CATEGORIES OF CONSUMER PRODUCTS

In addition to categorising by type of offering, most products intended for consumer use can be further categorised by how frequently and where they are purchased.

- *Convenience products*: These are products that appeal to a very large market segment. They are generally consumed regularly and purchased frequently. Examples include most household items such as food, cleaning products, and personal care products. Because of the high purchase volume, pricing per item tends to be relatively low and consumers often see little value in shopping around since additional effort yields minimal savings. From the marketer's perspective the low price of convenience products means that profit per unit sold is very low. In order to make high profits marketers must sell in large volume. Consequently, marketers attempt to distribute these products in mass through as many retail outlets as possible.

– *Shopping products:* These are products which consumers purchase and consume on a less frequent schedule compared to convenience products. Consumers are willing to spend more time locating these products since they are relatively more expensive than convenience products and because these may possess additional psychological benefits for the purchaser, such as raising their perceived status level within their social group. Examples include many clothing products, personal services, electronic products, and household furnishings. Because consumers are purchasing less frequently and are willing to shop to locate these products, the target market is much smaller than that of convenience goods. Consequently, marketers often are more selective when choosing distribution outlets to sell their products.

– *Speciality products:* These are products that tend to carry a high price tag relative to convenience and shopping products. Consumption may occur at about the same rate as shopping products but consumers are much more selective. In fact, in many cases consumers know in advance which product they prefer and will not shop to compare products. But they may shop at retailers that provide the best value. Examples include high-end luxury automobiles, expensive champagne, and celebrity hair care experts. The target markets are generally very small and outlets selling the products are very limited to the point of being exclusive.

In addition to the three main categories above, products are classified in at least two additional ways:

- *Emergency products:* These are products a customer seeks due to sudden events and for which pre-purchase planning is not considered. Often the decision is one of convenience (e.g., whatever works to fix a problem) or personal fulfilment (e.g., perceived to improve purchaser's image).
- *Unsought products:* These are products whose purchase is unplanned by the consumer but occur as a result of marketer's actions. Such purchase decisions are made when the customer is exposed to promotional activity, such as a salesperson's persuasion or purchase incentives like special discounts offered to certain online shoppers. These promotional activities often lead customers to engage in Impulse Purchasing.

CATEGORIES OF BUSINESS PRODUCTS

Products sold within the b-to-b market fall into one of the following categories:

- *Raw materials*: These are products obtained through mining, harvesting, fishing, etc., that are key ingredients in the production of higher-order products.
- *Processed materials*: These are products created through the processing of basic raw materials. In some cases the processing refines original raw materials while in other cases the process combines different raw materials to create something new. For instance, several crops including corn and sugar cane can be processed to create ethanol which has many uses including as a fuel to power car and truck engines.

- *Equipment:* These are products used to help with production or operations activities. Examples range from conveyor belts used on an assembly line to large buildings used to house the headquarters staff of a multi-national company.
- *Basic components:* These are products used within more advanced components. These are often built with raw material or processed material. Electrical wire is an example.
- *Advanced components:* These are products that use basic components to produce products that offer a significant function needed within a larger product. Yet by itself an advanced component does not stand alone as a final product. In computers the motherboard would be an example since it contains many basic components but without the inclusion of other products would have little value.
- *Product component:* These are products used in the assembly of a final product though these could also function as stand alone products. Dice included as part of a children's board game would be an example.
- *MRO (Maintenance, Repair and Operating) Products:* These are products used to assist with the operation of the organisation but are not directly used in producing goods or services. Office supplies, parts for a truck fleet and natural gas to heat a factory would fall into this category.

COMPONENTS OF A PRODUCT

On the surface it seems a product is simply a marketing offering, whether tangible or intangible, that someone wants to purchase and consume. In which case one might believe product decisions are focused exclusively on designing and building the consumable elements of goods, services or ideas. For instance, one might think the key product decision for a manufacturer of floor cleaners is to focus on creating a formula that cleans more effectively. In actuality, while decisions related to the consumable parts of the product are extremely important, the total product consists of more than what is consumed. The total product offering and the decisions facing the marketer can be broken down into three key parts:

- Core benefits.
- Actual product.
- Augmented product.

Core Benefits

While many needs are addressed by the consumption of a product or service, some needs are not. For instance, customers may need to be perceived highly by other members of their group or need a product that is easy to use or need a risk-free purchase. In each of these cases, and many more, the core product itself is the benefit the customer receives from using the product. In some cases these core benefits are offered by the product itself (e.g., floor cleaner) while in other cases the benefit is offered by other aspects of the product (e.g., the can containing the floor cleaner that makes it easier to spread the product). Consequently, at the very heart of all product decisions is determining the key or core benefits a product will provide. From this decision, the rest of the product offering can be developed.

Actual Product

The core benefits are offered through the components that make up the actual product the customer purchases. For instance, when a consumer returns home from shopping at the grocery store and takes a purchased item out of her shopping bag, the actual product is the item she holds in her hand. Within the actual product is the consumable product, which can be viewed as the main good, service or idea the customer is buying. For instance, while toothpaste may come in a package that makes dispensing it easy, the Consumable Product is the paste that is placed on a toothbrush. But marketers must understand that while the consumable product is, in most cases, the most critical of all product decisions, the actual product includes many separate product decisions including product features, branding, packaging, labelling, and more.

Augmented Product

Marketers often surround their actual products with goods and services that provide additional value to the customer's purchase. While these factors may not be key reasons leading customers to purchase (i.e., not core benefits), for some the inclusion of these items strengthens the purchase decision while for others failure to include these may cause the customer not to buy. Items considered part of the augmented product include:

- *Guarantee*: This provides a level of assurance that the product will perform up to expectations and if not the company marketing the product will support the customer's decision to replace, have it repaired or return for a refund.
- *Warranty*: This offers customers a level of protection that often extends past the guarantee period to cover repair or replacement of certain product components.
- *Customer service*: This consists of additional services that support the customer's needs including offering training and assistance via telephone or online.

— *Complementary products*: The value of some product purchases can be enhanced with add-on products, such as items that make the main product easier to use (e.g., laptop carrybag), enhance styling (e.g., cellphone face plates) or extend functionality (e.g., portable keyboard for PDAs).

— *Accessibility*: How customers obtain the product can affect its perceived value depending on such considerations as how easy it is to obtain (e.g., stocked at nearby store, delivered directly to office), the speed at which it can be obtained, and the likelihood it will be available when needed.

KEY PRODUCT DECISIONS

The actual product is designed to provide the core benefits sought by the target market. The marketer offers these benefits through a combination of factors that make up the actual product.

There are four key factors that together help shape the actual product. These factors include:

— Consumable product features.

— Branding.

— Packaging.

— Labelling.

Decisions regarding the product, price, promotion and distribution channels are decisions on the elements of the "marketing mix". It can be argued that product decisions are probably the most crucial as the product is the very epitome of marketing planning. Errors in product decisions are legion. These can include the imposition of a global standardised product where it is inapplicable, for example large horsepower tractors may be totally unsuitable for areas where small scale farming exists and where incomes are low; devolving decisions to affiliated countries which may let quality slip; and the attempt to sell products into a country without cognisance of cultural adaptation needs. The decision whether to sell globally standardised or adapted products is too simplistic for today's market place. Many product decisions lie between these two extremes. Cognisance has also to be taken of the stage in the international life cycle, the organisation's own product portfolio, its strengths and weaknesses and its global objectives. Unfortunately, most developing countries are in no position to compete on the world stage with many manufactured value-added products. Quality, or lack of it, is often the major letdown.

In decisions on producing or providing products and services in the international market it is essential that the production of the product or service is well planned and coordinated, both within and with other functional area of the firm, particularly marketing. For example, in horticulture, it is essential that any supplier or any of his "outgrower" (sub-contractor) can supply what he says he can. This is especially vital when contracts for supply are finalised, as failure to supply could incur large penalties. The main elements to consider are the production process itself, specifications, culture, the physical product, packaging, labelling, branding, warranty and service.

The key question is, can we ensure continuity of supply? In manufactured products this may include decisions on the type of manufacturing process—artisanal, job, batch, flow line or group technology.

Quantity and quality of horticultural crops are affected by a number of things. These include input supplies (or lack of them), finance and credit availability, variety (choice), sowing dates, product range and investment advice. Many of these items will be catered for in the contract of supply.

Specification

Specification is very important. Some markets will not take produce unless it is within their specification. Specifications are often set by the customer, but agents, standard authorities and trade associations can be useful sources. Quality requirements often vary considerably.

Culture

Product packaging, labeling, physical characteristics and marketing have to adapt to the cultural requirements when necessary. Religion, values, aesthetics, language and material culture all affect production decisions.

Physical Product

The physical product is made up of a variety of elements. These elements include the physical product and the subjective image of the product. Consumers are looking for benefits and these must be conveyed in the total product package. Physical characteristics include range, shape, size, colour, quality, quantity and compatibility. Subjective attributes are determined by advertising, self image, labelling and packaging. In manufacturing or selling produce, cognisance has to be taken of cost and country legal requirements.

Packaging

Packaging serves many purposes. It protects the product from damage which could be incurred in handling and transportation and also has a promotional aspect. It can be very expensive. Size, unit type, weight and volumes are very important in packaging. For aircraft cargo the package needs to be light but strong, for sea cargo containers are often the best form. The customer may also decide the best form of packaging. In horticultural produce, the developed countries often demand blister packs for mangetouts, beans, strawberries and so on, whilst for products like pineapples a sea container may suffice. Costs of packaging have always to be weighed against the advantage gained by it.

Final customer packaging is the package, the final customer receives in exchange for their payment. When the final customer makes a purchase he or she is initially exposed to the primary package—the outermost container that is seen and touched by the final customer. This primary package can be further divided into the following:

- *First-Level package:* This is packaging that holds the actual product. In some cases this packaging is minimal since it only serves to protect the product. For instance, certain frozen food products are sold to consumers in a cardboard box with the product itself contained in a plastic bag found inside the box. This plastic bag represents the first-level package. In other cases frozen food products are sold in the plastic bag that contains the product. In these cases the plastic bag is both first-level package and the primary package for convey product information.
- *Second-level package:* In some cases the first-level package is surrounded by one or more outer packages. This second-level package may act as the primary package for the product.
- *Package inserts:* Marketers use a variety of other methods to communicate with customers after they open the product package. These methods are often inserted within, or sometimes on, the product's package. Insertions include information such as instruction manuals and warranty cards,

promotional incentives such as coupons, and items that add value such as recipes and software.

Labelling

Labelling not only serves to express the contents of the product, but may be promotional. India is now putting very stringent regulations in force on labelling, even to the degree that the pesticides and insecticides used on horticultural produce have to be listed. This could be very demanding for producers, especially small scale, ones where production techniques may not be standardised. Government labelling regulations vary from country to country. Bar codes are not widespread in Africa, but do assist in stock control. Labels may have to be multilingual, especially if the product is a world brand. Translation could be a problem with many words being translated with difficulty. Again labelling is expensive, and in promotion terms non-standard labels are more expensive than standard ones. Requirements for crate labelling, etc. for international transportation will be dealt with later under documentation.

Product Naming

Product naming is the discipline of deciding what a product will be called, and is very similar in concept and approach to the process of deciding on a name for a company or organisation. Product naming is considered a critical part of the branding process, which includes all of the marketing activities that affect the brand image, such as positioning and the design of logo, packaging and the product itself. Product naming involves the application of creative and linguistic strategy and results in a brand name that becomes a product's shorthand.

The process involved in product naming can take months or years to complete. Some key steps include specifying the objectives of the branding, developing the product name itself, evaluating names through target market testing and focus groups, choosing a final product name, and finally identifying it as a trademark it for protection.

Trademarks

A consideration companies find important in developing a product name is its "trade-markability." Product name trademarks may be established in a number of ways:

- In many countries, including the United States, names can be used as trademarks without formal registration through first use or common law—simply to protect an established product's name and reputation.
- Product names can be formally registered within a state, with protection limited to that state's borders.
- The preeminent system for registering international trademarks in multiple jurisdictions is the Madrid system.

In addition, protecting a trademark is just as important as the initial process of registration. Trademark rights are maintained through actual use of the trademark, and will diminish over time if a trademark is not actively used.

Branding

Branding involves decisions that establish an identity for a product with the goal of distinguishing it from competitors' offerings. In markets where competition is fierce and where customers may select from among many competitive products, creating an identity through branding is essential. It is particularly important in helping position the product in the minds of the product's target market.

While consumer products companies have long recognised the value of branding, it has only been within the last 10-15 years that organisations selling component products in the business-to-business market have begun to focus on brand building strategies. The most well-known company to brand components is Intel with its now famous "Intel Inside" slogan. Intel's success has led many other b-to-b companies and even non-profits to incorporate branding within their overall marketing strategy.

Warranty

Many large value products like machinery require warranties. Unfortunately not everyone upholds them. It is common practice in India that if the original equipment has not been bought through an authorised dealer in the country, that dealer refuses to honour the warranty. This is unfortunate, because not only may the equipment have been legitimately bought overseas, it also actually builds up consumer resistance to the dealer. When the consumer is eventually offered a choice, the reticent. dealer will suffer.

11
MARKETING MANAGEMENT

Marketing management is a business discipline which is focused on the practical application of marketing techniques and the management of a firm's marketing resources and activities. Marketing managers are often responsible for influencing the level, timing, and composition of customer demand accepted definition of the term. In part, this is because the role of a marketing manager can vary significantly based on a business' size, corporate culture, and industry context. For example, in a large consumer products company, the marketing manager may act as the overall general manager of his or her assigned product.

From this perspective, the scope of marketing management is quite broad. The implication of such a definition is that any activity or resource the firm uses to acquire customers and manage the company's relationships with them is within the purview of marketing management.

MARKETING RESEARCH AND ANALYSIS

In order to make fact-based decisions regarding marketing strategy and design effective, cost-efficient implementation programmes, firms must possess a detailed, objective understanding of their own business and the market in which they operate. In analysing these issues, the discipline of marketing management often overlaps with the related discipline of strategic planning.

Traditionally, marketing analysis was structured into three areas: Customer analysis, Company analysis, and Competitor analysis. More recently, it has become fashionable in some marketing circles to divide these further into certain five "Cs": Customer analysis, Company analysis, Collaborator analysis, Competitor analysis, and analysis of the industry Context.

The focus of customer analysis is to develop a scheme for market segmentation, breaking down the market into various constituent groups of customers, which are called customer segments or market segments. Marketing managers work to develop detailed profiles of each segment, focusing on any number of variables that may differ among the segments: demographic, psychographic, geographic, behavioural, needs-benefit, and other factors may all be examined. Marketers also attempt to track these segments' perceptions of the various products in the market using tools such as perceptual mapping.

In company analysis, marketers focus on understanding the company's cost structure and cost position relative to competitors, as well as working to identify a firm's core competencies and other competitively distinct company resources. Marketing managers may also work with the accounting department to analyse the profits the firm is generating from various product lines and customer accounts. The company may also conduct periodic brand audits to assess the strength of its brands and sources of brand equity.

The firm's collaborators may also be profiled, which may include various suppliers, distributors and other channel partners, joint venture partners, and others. An analysis of complementary products may also be performed if such products exist.

Marketing management employs various tools from economics and competitive strategy to analyse the industry context in which the firm operates. These include Porter's five forces, analysis of strategic groups of competitors, value chain analysis and others. Depending on the industry, the regulatory context may also be important to examine in detail.

In Competitor analysis, marketers build detailed profiles of each competitor in the market, focusing especially on their relative competitive strengths and weaknesses using SWOT analysis. Marketing managers will examine each competitor's cost structure, sources of profits, resources and competencies, competitive positioning and product differentiation, degree of vertical integration, historical responses to industry developments, and other factors.

Marketing management often finds it necessary to invest in research to collect the data required to perform accurate marketing analysis. As such, they often conduct market research (alternately marketing research) to obtain this information. Marketers employ a variety of techniques to conduct market research, but some of the more common include:

- Qualitative marketing research, such as focus groups.
- Quantitative marketing research, such as statistical surveys.
- Experimental techniques such as test markets.
- Observational techniques such as ethnographic observation.

Marketing managers may also design and oversee various environmental scanning and competitive intelligence processes to help identify trends and inform the company's marketing analysis.

MARKETING STRATEGY

Once the company has obtained an adequate understanding of the customer base and its own competitive position in the industry, marketing managers are able to make key strategic decisions and develop a marketing strategy designed to maximise the revenues and profits of the firm. The selected strategy may aim for any of a variety of specific objectives, including optimising short-term unit margins, revenue growth, market share, long-term profitability, or other goals.

To achieve the desired objectives, marketers typically identify one or more target customer segments which they intend to pursue. Customer segments are often selected as targets because they score highly on two dimensions:

(a) The segment is attractive to serve because it is large, growing, makes frequent purchases, is not price sensitive (i.e. is willing to pay high prices), or other factors; and

(b) The company has the resources and capabilities to compete for the segment's business, can meet their needs better than the competition, and can do so profitably. In fact, a commonly cited definition of marketing is simply "meeting needs profitably."

The implication of selecting target segments is that the business will subsequently allocate more resources to acquire and retain customers in the target segment(s) than it will for other, non-targeted customers. In some cases, the firm may go so far as to turn away customers that are not in its target segment. The doorman at a swanky nightclub, for example, may deny entry to unfashionably dressed individuals because the business has made a strategic decision to target the "high fashion" segment of nightclub patrons.

In conjunction with targeting decisions, marketing managers will identify the desired positioning they want the company, product, or brand to occupy in the target customer's mind. This positioning is often an encapsulation of a key benefit the company's product or service offers that is differentiated and superior to the benefits offered by competitive products.

Ideally, a firm's positioning can be maintained over a long period of time because the company possesses, or can develop, some form of sustainable competitive advantage. The positioning should also be sufficiently relevant to the target segment such that it will drive the purchasing behaviour of target customers.

IMPLEMENTATION PLANNING

After the firm's strategic objectives have been identified, the target market selected, and the desired positioning for the company, product or brand has been determined, marketing managers focus on how to best implement the chosen strategy. Traditionally, this has involved implementation planning across the "four P's" of marketing:

1. Product management,
2. Pricing,
3. Place (i.e. sales and distribution channels), and
4. Promotion.

Taken together, the company's implementation choices across the four P's are often described as the marketing mix, meaning the mix of elements the business will employ to "go to market" and execute the marketing strategy. The overall goal for the marketing mix is to consistently deliver a compelling value proposition that reinforces the firm's chosen positioning, builds customer loyalty and brand equity among target customers, and achieves the firm's marketing and financial objectives.

In many cases, marketing management will develop a marketing plan to specify how the company will execute the chosen strategy and achieve the business' objectives. The content of marketing plans varies from firm to firm, but commonly includes:

- An executive summary;
- Situation analysis to summarise facts and insights gained from market research and marketing analysis;
- The company's mission statement or long-term strategic vision;
- A statement of the company's key objectives, often subdivided into marketing objectives and financial objectives;
- The marketing strategy the business has chosen, specifying the target segments to be pursued and the competitive positioning to be achieved;
- Implementation choices for each element of the marketing mix (the four P's).

BIBLIOGRAPHY

Aaker, D and Joachimsthaler, E., *Brand Leadership*, The Free Press, 2000.

Hoyer, W.D. and MacInnis, D.J., *Consumer Behaviour*, 2nd Edition, USA: Houghton Mifflin Company, 2001.

Baker, M., *Marketing Management and Strategy*, 3rd edition, Macmillan Business, 2000.

Blythe, J., *Essentials of Marketing*, 2nd edition, Prentice Hall, 2001.

Brassington, F and Pettitt, S, *Principles of Marketing*, Second Edition, Prentice Hall, Harlow, 2000.

Chris Murray, *The Marketing Gurus: Lessons from the Best Marketing Books of All Time*, Portfolio Hardcover, 2006.

Chisnall, P.M., *Marketing Research*, Fifth Edition, London: McGraw-Hill, 1997.

David Meerman Scott , *The New Rules of Marketing and PR: How to Use News Releases, Blogs, Podcasting, Viral Marketing and Online Media to Reach Buyers Directly*, Wiley, 2007.

Davies, M., *Understanding Marketing*, 1st edition. Prentice Hall, 1998.

Ellwood, I., *The Essential Brand book*, Kogan Page Limited, 2002.

Fill, C., *Marketing Communications, Contexts, strategies and applications*, Prentice Hall, 2002.

Kapferer, J., *Strategic Brand Management*, Kogan Page, 1997.

Keller, K., *Strategic Brand Management, Building, measuring and managing brand equity*, Kogan Page, London, 1998.

Kotler, P, Armstrong, G, Saunders, J and Wong, V, *Principles of Marketing*, Third European Edition, Prentice Hall, Harlow, 2001.

Kotler, P. and Armstrong, G., *Marketing An Introduction*, Fourth Edition. New Jersey. Prentince Hall International, 1997.

Kotler, P., Armstrong, G., Saunders, J. and Wong, V., *Principles of Marketing*, 2nd Edition, New Jersey: Prentice Hall, 1999.

Linneman, R.E. and Stanton, J.L., *Making Niche Marketing Work*, New York: McGraw HIll, 1991.

Loudon, D.L. and Della Bitta, A.J., *Consumer Behaviour*, 4th Edition, USA: McGraw Hill, 1993.

Lovelock, *Services Marketing, people, technology, strategy*, Prentice Hall, 2001.

Lury, G., *Brand Watching; lifting the lid on the phenomena of branding*, Blackhall, 1998.

McDonald, M., *Marketing Plans. How to prepare them, how to use the*, 4th edition, Butterworth Heinenamm, 2001.

Nirmalya, Kumar, *Marketing As Strategy: Understanding The Ceo's Agenda For Driving Growth And Innovation*, Penguin, India, 2006.

Proctor, T., *Essentials of Marketing research*, UK: Financial Times-Prentice Hall, 2000.

Randall, G., *Principles of Marketing*, 2nd edition, Thomson Learning, 2001.

Van Auken, B., *The Brand Management Checklist*, Kogan Page, 2002.

Weilbacher, W., "Brand Marketing: Building winning brand strategies that deliver value and customer satisfaction", *chapter1 and* 2, NTC business books, 1993.

Ziethmal, & Bitner, "Services Marketing: integrating customer focus across the firm", *chapters 1,3 and 6*, McGraw Hill, 2003.